In the Stillness

A Prayer Journey

to

Hearing the Voice of God

by

Caron Massey

In the Stillness
By Caron Massey

ISBN: 978-1-7375320-0-2

Printed by DiggyPOD, Inc., in the United States of America. First printing, 2021.

Cover Photo by Joel Cross on Unsplash.com

Scripture quotations are from The Lockman Foundation, *New American Standard Bible* (NASB) or (NASB1995).

Mike & Caron Massey
Winchester, KY

Caron@IntheStillness.org

www.InTheStillness.org

Contents

In the Stillness

Dedication

To Author, Mentor, and friend Margaret Therkelsen, without her telling me to write a book, there wouldn't be one. Heaven has her now, but we'll see each other for eternity.

To my husband Mike, your steadfast unconditional love and unwavering faith mean everything to me. I'm so grateful for you and love you beyond words.

To my Son's and their wives, Micah and Jayme, Jonah and Hope, and my son Malachi. Thank you all for encouraging me to write, to not give up, and to keep my focus on Jesus. What a joy you are in my life. I love you all so very much.

Introduction

I want to begin by saying that this little book has been in the making for way too long. Everyday life tends to get in the way, so procrastination and disbelief set in. I have repented to the Lord for both of these, and refuse to allow any more time to pass.

I am reminded of the story in Genesis of Sarah and Abraham. Sarah received a promise from God to give her a son, but she didn't believe it because of her age. Sarah even tried to bring forth the promise through her servant Hagar, who did birth a son, but the act was not of the Lord. Still, the Lord in His goodness blessed Hagar's son Ishmael anyway. I compare Sarah to myself. I've struggled with believing that the Lord could use me through my heart's desire for writing. The enemy will always target our minds with insecurities in order to rob us of our gifts and callings. The devil is a loser and tries to drag us down with him.

One time, years ago, my family and I were standing in the kitchen and I shared with them that the Holy Spirit wanted me to write a book on prayer and having a relationship with Him. I said that there were so many books already on this subject and there wasn't a need for another one. My son Micah, who was age 13 at the time, said jokingly, "Yeah Mom, because the God of the universe can't possibly say anything new through YOU!"

I was stopped in my tracks, lovingly rebuked by the Lord through my son. I was reminded that anything that comes through me for the Kingdom of God has nothing to do with me; it is all about Jesus. My prideful self-doubt was basically telling God that He didn't know what He was doing to put a book on my heart to write. As I have yielded through more repentance, it has still taken me years to "birth" this book, but I decided I would be obedient to complete it no matter how long it took. I'm sure Sarah and some of you can relate. In the same way that my oldest son Micah rebuked me, my middle son Jonah now gives me the constant reminder, "Mom, write your book!" Won't they be surprised to finally read it.

Prayer is a passion for me. I have been blessed to be a part of many circles of prayer, and also lead some. These circles have included people of all denominations and nationalities, but we were all unified through our hearts for prayer and corporate intercession. Prayer is a journey that allows us to hear the voice of God. Most people do not believe they can hear the Lord speak. In this book I will show you how we can.

I believe there are many of God's people who have been given a passion and a promise by the Lord, but who are still waiting to walk in that promise. Perhaps you are one of them. You've clearly heard a desire in your heart rise up that you know is bigger than yourself, or maybe you have yet to step into that promise or desire. It is time to believe it, yield to it, claim it, and do it.

I pray as you read this little book on prayer, while having a relationship with Jesus and listening for his voice, that you realize God loves you and stands by what He tells you. He restores what time has been robbed from us and what the locusts have eaten, and can launch His promise through us at any moment. All we need to do is spend time with Him and believe that He can do it. No matter what our calling or journey with the Lord is, it all starts with prayer and sitting at His feet. This book is not profound in any way -- it may even be repetitive for many who read it -- but with open hearts, we can always be encouraged and find something worth receiving. Be blessed!

In the Stillness

1 – Relatable God

Although He was a Son, He learned obedience from the things which He suffered. – Hebrews 5:8

You may already have a prayer life with God. Here are a few questions... How deep is your relationship with Him? Do you talk with Him daily? Are you a student of the Word or do you simply read it? Can you hear Him speaking to you?

The whole point of a relationship with God is so we can hear Him, receive His love and pour it back onto Him and out to others. Hearing God's voice is something that we all have done, but did we recognize His voice when He spoke to us?

Did you ever wonder why it was in God's divine plan to bring Jesus to us as a baby, a helpless infant that needed a mother and father to care for him? Why didn't He just descend from heaven, as He ascended?

I believe it was God's grace and mercy to show us the personhood of Jesus. He chose to come as a vulnerable baby, in total reliance upon the Father's protection, provision, and direction. It was to show us that we can relate to Jesus as a baby, a child, a teenager, and man of God. He was born a baby and lived a life, just as we come into the world to live our lives. Jesus walked the earth just long enough to fall madly in love with us and build relationships with those around Him. He knew His life would take him to the Cross on our behalf.

I think some of us believe Jesus went to the Cross because, well, He was Jesus, and that it wasn't as hard for Him because of who He was. Actually, Jesus loved us more than we can imagine. The Word says He "learned" obedience (Hebrews 5:8).

Jesus is the example for us all so we can choose daily not to sin. He was tempted like we are tempted. In the desert he was tempted to the very depths of his capabilities and power, yet He still chose to lay down His rights and take upon Himself the sins of the entire world. (1 John 2:2). He suffered and so will we.

Jesus died for the darkest evil that exists in man. His death and resurrection canceled that evil -- broke its power -- so that we might have life eternal. Can we possibly imagine, or comprehend? It was the perfect counter attack against the enemy's plan for all mankind.

We see that the life, death, and resurrection of Jesus took place not only to save our necks, but also so we could relate to Him (on some level) as a person. After His death the very personhood of Jesus returned to us by His Spirit and lives within those who choose to receive Him. Our ability to relate to Him becomes the stepping stone to our true identity.

Do you remember the moment you knew you would give your life to Jesus? The first time you heard His voice? Maybe not audibly, but certainly you felt the tugging on your heart to receive His life and ask Him into yours? The Holy Spirit spoke long ago over His creation and still hovers over us, both audibly and otherwise. He spoke the world into existence (Genesis 1).

When it comes to pondering having a relationship with the triune God -- the Father, Son and Holy Spirit -- the idea can seem a bit mysterious and certainly underrated. I believe this is because not one person has the capability of truly explaining a deep relationship with Him.

The reason this can be difficult is because it's personal. No matter how much you read the Bible or all the books out there, nothing can tell you what your own relationship and experience with Jesus is supposed to be like. It sounds like we are all just aspiring to be good Christians who pray and get a prompting here and there to go this way or that, but it's so much more. His plan is to have a one-of-a-kind relationship with *you*, a relationship as unique as your fingerprint, that is shared only between you and Him and that is not like anyone else's. Do you believe you are this special?

Maybe you have just enough of a relationship with Jesus to be satisfied. Maybe you think it's as good as it gets. Maybe you are frustrated and numb in your walk with God. Are you just going through the motions as a good Christian is supposed to do, praying your daily prayers and reading your Bible? There is nothing wrong with these habits if you sense real growth happening in your soul and a real prayer relationship with God developing daily. If you are stagnant and stuck, then let's pull you up and out of that circumstance to begin again!

There are many books on prayer and having a personal relationship with God, but not many on hearing His voice. As my son Micah so kindly reminded me, there is always more that the Lord wants to share from the depths of His heart with us. The ultimate goal of being a Spirit-filled Christian is not only to have an active and powerful walk with the Lord, but to be able to hear His voice speaking to us and directing us. He has many ways to speak to us, all of them are powerful -- His Word, His people, His creation, and the circumstances we experience. God speaks through them all.

The question is not, "Can you hear God's voice?" The question is, "Do you believe He is speaking to you?"

Hearing the voice of God, for most of us, is a journey of building confidence over time spent with the Lord in the stillness of obedience to Him. As we spend time with Him, He woos us and nudges our hearts, speaking quietly in new and different ways.

One time when I was in high school, I was trying to break up with my boyfriend, who sang in a youth choir with me. I wanted my "space." I told him I was breaking up with him and he said, "No." I said, "What?" He said that he had prayed to the Lord that I would be his wife and that he believed we were to be married. First of all, "no" was a fighting word to me and second, those who know me will tell you that I'm a pretty feisty person. So my reply to his statement shocked me as much as it did my boyfriend. I replied with, "Okay." The reason I responded that way was because as I heard him tell me that he had prayed for me and that I was his, I heard the voice of the Lord within my spirit say, "I want you to marry him." It was a pivotal moment in my life and I knew it. I was humbled instantly, so I said, "Okay." I'm sure all of heaven shook.

When I look back at it, I'm amazed at the courage and faith of my now husband Mike. He knew I was to be his wife and he spoke it out to me with such boldness of faith. Now, thirty-four years later, I'm so very grateful he did, and grateful I listened to the Lord.

The Holy Spirit has unique things to say through each one of us about His own plans. The message is rarely about us, but about Him and His Kingdom.

In relating to the Lord and hearing His voice, we first have to see in the Word God's personhood and deity. He is real. Many think of God as this mighty being who throws down thunder bolts wherever He points His golden scepter and we'd better be good or else. Rather than a loving and caring God who knows us by name, we have fictionalized Him like the Greek god Zeus. Our life's experiences have gotten in the way of the truth and we feel we cannot relate to God. This is exactly what the devil wants us to think.

Let's look at some scriptures that will reveal how very real God is, and how his love and personal relationship are obtainable on many deep levels and layers.

Maybe you already have a good relationship with the Lord. Do you want to go deeper? We are called to sit with Him and get to know Him. "God is faithful, through whom you were called into fellowship with His Son, Jesus Christ our Lord." – 1 Corinthians 1:9

To fellowship with God is to associate with Him through His Son Jesus. None of us are too far advanced in our relationship with Jesus that we can't go deeper, not only with Him, but with the Father, too. Jesus said, "He who has seen Me has seen the Father." – John 14:9

Hearing the voice of God began in Genesis 1:1-25, where we read of God as Creator. In this passage, God is busy forming and making the earth. We see many times where after He creates something, he sees that "it was good." He spoke and it came into being. Life had to obey; creation heard and had to obey. It was formed out of obedience to His voice.

It's important to know that just as God's words are powerful enough to create, so are our words. We can either create a relationship with God and each other with our words, or we can create barriers to keep us apart. "The mouth of the righteous is a fountain of life, But the mouth of the wicked conceals violence." – Proverbs 10:11

Likewise, we can create evil as well as good with what we say. "The good person out of the good treasure of his heart brings forth what is good; and the evil person out of the evil treasure brings forth what is evil; for his mouth speaks from that which fills his heart." – Luke 6:45

Perhaps God didn't just speak us into existence, some believe He *sang* the whole earth into being. When we look at the narrative in the Hebrew language, "spirit" is RUACH, which means "breath." So, just as God breathed life into Adam, He breathed the earth into being. The belief that God sang us into being comes from the idea that He breathed life into Adam just as He spoke all creation into being. His breath, together with His voice, would be singing. Maybe they are one and the same. As everything in the earth is praising God, why couldn't He bring us forth with songs of joy? We are made in His image and we are beings of singing and rejoicing. Even the heavens sing.

"When the morning stars sang together and all the sons of God shouted for joy." – Job 38:7

So many believe that we cannot hear the Lord speak but the truth is, He spoke us into being a long time ago, and is still speaking. Just as He formed us in our mother's womb, the spoken word of truth and power hovers in the Spirit realm. It is never bound by time since time was created for us.

I remember when I first heard the Holy Spirit speaking to my spirit. I was seven years old and it was Resurrection Day/Easter Sunday and the pastor gave an altar call for salvation. He asked if anyone wanted Jesus to come into their lives, explaining that we could live forever in heaven and that it was a free gift. He invited anyone interested to come up to the altar. I got up out of my pew and walked up front. I remember feeling the tug on my heart, looking at my Mother, and knowing that I had to walk up front. Did I hear with my ears? No, but I certainly did with my spiritual ears. Do we normally hear with our ears what is being spoken to us in the Spirit by God? By Angels? No, but that doesn't mean we can't.

As I shared earlier, I believe the spoken Word of God in the very beginning of time is still hovering around us. "Heaven and earth will pass away, but My words will never pass away." – Matthew 24:35

All the promises that God has spoken over us and about us are swirling in the Spirit. Why can't we hear it? I believe some of the breakdown is our ability to relate to God, to know and understand His heart, and believe that He truly wants to be with us.

All of us, on some level, can relate to making something. We've made something we've liked and thought that it was good. These are the first verses in the Bible that show us how very relatable the personhood of God is. We know what it feels like to appreciate something we've made. We feel proud of it and want to share it with others. God is no different; He is a proud Creator and Father. As we are made in His image, our longing to share what we've made comes from Him.

In Genesis we read that God is not alone. "Let us make mankind in our image, according to Our likeness; and let them rule over the fish of the sea and of the birds of the sky and over the livestock and over all the earth, and over every crawling thing that crawls on the earth." – Genesis 1:26

In this verse we see the personhoods of God, His deity. It is the first indication that we can relate to God as not being alone but having someone with Him. This would be Jesus before he was born in the flesh, and the Holy Spirit.

If this concept is new to you, I encourage you as you read this book to have a little "mental shelf," where you can set new ideas or thoughts you aren't sure about. Then you can revisit them later. I've done this for years and it's truly helpful. Just because we may know something doesn't mean there isn't another layer of revelation for us. Or, there may be something said here that you totally disagree with, so put it on the shelf and see if it makes more sense later.

And so, since we read that God is using words like "Us" and "Our," we can see that He is not alone.

We can all relate to not wanting to be alone. In verse 27 we read where God creates man in His own image; he created male and female in His own image and told them to be fruitful and multiply. I believe this is a reference of being equal as male and female, at the foot of the Cross. We are both made in God's image so we are equally made but obviously with different roles. We are different but can certainly relate to one another. Though we are the spoken word of God, the Word incarnate was still to come. Still, we are part of the creation of God and He spoke us into being. I know this may not be new to you, or it might seem repetitive, but I am trying to drill this in.

On a little side note, I have been around long enough to see firsthand the misunderstandings that come with women teaching or being among the leadership in ministry. It has been a huge robbery and attack of the devil to cap women from being useful for the kingdom. The enemy has taken truth and twisted it. He knows we are both made in the image of God. If he can degrade one half of us, he knows that we won't be unified as the Bride of Christ. This is a direct attack against the prayers that Jesus prayed in John 17, that we would be one as He and the Father are one, so that the world would know Him. If we are not one, then the world continues on a path of disunity and destruction. It's sadly that simple.

For those who struggle with the men being head of the home and women being inferior, I have a question for you. Is there any part of God that is inferior to the rest of Him? Of course not. Just as the Holy Spirit has a different function than God the Father, they work together. It is the same for men and women. We are equal but with different roles for the Kingdom. By working together in love and humility, we can accomplish great things through the Holy Spirit. Still, the finished work was "good" in the eyes of God. As far as gender talk, that's for another book. I would recommend the book, Why Not Women? by Loren Cunningham and David Hamilton.

In Genesis 2:2 we read where "God completed the work He had done and rested on the 7th day." We can certainly relate to resting, but usually we associate rest with being tired. God was not tired; rather, the Hebrew word is NUACH, to be quiet, rest, cease, stopped.

In these verses the word *rest* means God had accomplished what He was doing, and was finished. What God created was good so He took time to delight in what He had made, all of creation including Man and Woman. What an amazing canvas He created.

In verse 3, God *blessed* the seventh day and sanctified it, which means he set it apart. This day of rest was obviously very important to God. He purposefully tells us that the seventh day is blessed by Him and set apart. It was sanctified, meant for resting, enjoyment, for the reflection and honoring of His completed work.

As God reflected on His week's work, so He wants us to do the same. To reflect on our time and how we spent it throughout the week can bring a heart of gratitude, or repentance, depending on how we conducted our week. Both are necessary. Here we can relate again to having something important in our lives, so important that we give it special attention and reflect on it. Having a new baby that we look at is a beautiful example. How would a normal couple feel about their new baby? They would adore it, cherish it, want to stare at it and ponder the beauty and details of what it looks like, reflecting on what they co-created with God.

This is how God feels about us and His world, though He didn't co-create anything, He did it all Himself. Later He would tell us to co-create with Him by going forth, multiplying, and subduing the earth.

God adores us, cherishes us and wants to care for us. Can you relate to God in His feelings over His creation? Of course you can. If there are misconceptions about God's character, or His love and care for you, hopefully there is a growing and new understanding happening in your heart and mind. God is good! His heart has always been to commune with us and be close to us. Some of us know this but may not fully believe it, for whatever reason. Maybe your hurts, wounds, religious mind sets, or daily schedules get in the way of truly accepting the fact that Jesus wants to spend time with you. That's okay. His love for you is not dependent upon what you think or do. It is constant and unconditional. What awesome news!

The purpose of going through these beginning scriptures is to spur us on and bring us closer to God's heart, then we can understand that having a deep intimate relationship with Him and hearing His voice is totally obtainable and not just something we've gotten used to hearing about. It was His original design that we would want to be near Him and relate to His love for us as we love Him.

As a Christian, to hear the voice of the Lord is a fundamental right. Many would say that we can't really hear Him speak but I say they are completely wrong. God's word says, "My sheep hear My voice, and I know them, and they follow Me." – John 10:27

God is not going to tell us something like this if it were not possible for us to do. It truly could not be any clearer that we are totally capable of hearing Him speak to us.

I know, I know, some of you are thinking, "Well I can't hear Him speak to me. Why can't I hear Him?" I want to reassure you that you can hear the Lord speaking to you as He speaks in many ways. You just have to make sure you are paying attention. Hallelujah!

2 – We Love Because He First Loved Us

See how great a love the Father has given us that we would be called children of God; and in fact we are. For this reason the world does not know us: because it did not know Him. – 1 John 3:1

Jesus was asked what commandment was the greatest, and He said, "'Love the Lord your God with all your heart, and with all your soul, and with all your mind.' This is the first and the greatest commandment. And the second is like it: 'Love your neighbor as yourself.' All the Law of the Prophets hang on these two commandments." – Matthew 22:36-40

God is saying the rest of the law doesn't matter if this is not being practiced. Paul calls us "sounding gongs" if we are not loving. (1 Corinthians 13:1)

Loving Jesus is the greatest thing I can practice and hope to obtain. I say practice, because how many of us can say that when we first received Jesus into our hearts and lives that we automatically loved Him? We joined ourselves to Him because we knew we needed Him. In the fear of the Lord, out of our need, we cried out to Him.

For us to love our spouse, friend, or neighbor it is the same. Usually, a relationship has to grow into truly loving someone. I say usually because through divine Agape love, we can love anyone -- even our enemies (see Matthew 5:44).

The Greek word *agape* refers to the highest form of love; this comes from God. It is His capabilities, not ours. Unconditional love has no end. It is absolutely possible for us to enter into agape love. As we surrender our heart and soul to Him, He allows us to do miraculous things. Loving others with an agape love is nothing short of a miracle. We can love at first sight or sight unseen through the Lord; we can love people the way He does if we only allow Him to love through us.

Our relationship with Jesus is no different in that it takes an investment of our time and energy. As we practice our relationship with Him, He begins to reveal more and more of His personhood to us. We begin to fall in love with Him. He so wants to become part of our daily lives and routines. He wants us to ask Him questions and make decisions with Him. Daily inclusion of the Holy Spirit in our lives results in hearing His voice even in the small things in life. We have to remember that our first mission in life is to minister to Jesus, learning to love Him and be loved by Him. It's a beautiful courtship.

It's not the same for Jesus towards us. He already loves us passionately, and that passion took Him to the Cross to die for us. Our relationship with Him is mostly a one-sided need, our side, our need. Yet Jesus desires our companionship and conversations, just like the ones we enjoy in a real person-to-person love relationship. This is what Jesus wants from us.

I remember when I was learning to treat Jesus like a person in my everyday life, as if He was always right next to me. I was driving home from work one day and felt His strong presence sitting next to me in the passenger seat. Did I see Him? No, but I knew the Holy Spirit was there. As I acknowledged Him in the car and began to pray and thank Him, in an act of faith, I reached over with my hand and placed it on the seat as if reaching out to touch Him. I did not FEEL Jesus in the natural, but I did in the Spirit. You might find this silly, strange or foreign, but it is very REAL when the Holy Spirit begins to show us He is with us and near us in the Spirit every day. It's a powerful revelation to know how real He is.

It is in these moments of faith and in deep communion with Jesus that we begin to touch our true identity. Our identity is all about Him and being in Him and in His perfect divine love.

"We have seen and testify that the Father has sent the Son of God, God abides in him, and he in God. We have come to know and have believed the love which God has for us. God is love, and the one who abides in love abides in God, and God abides in him. By this, love is perfected with us, so that we may have confidence in the Day of Judgment; because as He is, so also are we in this world. There is no fear in love; but perfect love casts out fear, because fear involves punishment, and the one who fears is not perfected in love. We love, because He first loved us." – 1 John 4:16-19

To love the Lord is to dwell with Him and to allow Him to dwell within us. As these scriptures say, we "rely" on the love God has for us which is through the Holy Spirit, the personhood of Jesus. The only way love can be made complete in us and the only way we can be like Jesus, is for us to rely on Him. When we rely on someone, we depend on them to help us in our need. We trust them without question. To allow these transactions within our relationship with Jesus is to love Him. It goes on to say "There is no fear in love," "perfect love casts out fear." This is so huge. Think about the many times you have been fearful in your life. Maybe now you are dealing with a situation that has you gripped with fear. Illness? Finances? Relationship? Death? Fear *can't* dwell where love is, as it must be cast out. It doesn't say fear is asked politely to leave, it says it's *cast out*! Here we see that God's perfect love protects us from fear. It throws out of us that which the enemy has spoken into our minds and hearts. This too is part of allowing Him to love us, which in return, is also loving Him back. As we are in this love relationship with Jesus, He enables us to love others as we should.

As we love Jesus, all things are promised to work for our good as in Romans 8:28. How sad it would be to not have the Lord in our lives: no hope, no love in the purest form.

In the Stillness

3 – Being Still

Be still and know that I am God; I will be exalted among the nations, I will be exalted in the earth. – Psalms 46:10

Being still is not natural for any of us, but it is a practice that we can learn to develop and a posture that is essential if we want a relationship with Jesus and an active prayer life with Him. If I could pick one verse in my life that the Lord, over time, has woven throughout my soul, it would be Psalm 46:10. It is this verse where the Lord began to reveal His heart to me, and show me who He is. There is a reaction that occurs from the first part of the verse to the latter and it all has to do with real discipleship. Out of being still with Him and becoming His disciple, and only then, is the Gospel taken to the nations in love and with power. I'll share more on this later.

I wish I could say that prayer has always been an exciting thing for me but the truth is, when I first started a daily prayer life, it was a huge chore. I didn't know how to be still. I was 18 and my future mother-in-law took me to a prayer group at our church. Little did I know it would take me on a never-ending journey of excitement and adventure.

At first, trying to learn to pray was just awkward and uncomfortable. The prayer group was led by author, teacher, speaker, and counselor Margaret Therkelsen. She began to mentor and counsel me as she did so many others. She was such a gift in my life. Margaret walked me through many questions and trials, always encouraging me to stay in the word, pray, and write daily. Well, I was never good at writing daily and I'm still a work in progress, but I'm so grateful that she pressed me to continue. I was the youngest in the prayer group. Most of the women were much older and very seasoned prayer warriors. I began attending the group regularly, and listened to the women pray every Tuesday for years. Margaret taught through contemplative prayer and Lectio Divina (more on that later).

Before doing anything else, Margaret always started us off with joyful worship, praise, and prayers of thanksgiving. Prayers of repentance always followed as our hearts were tender after corporate worship. Margaret played the piano like a swan on a lake. I can see her now; she was tall, had a long elegant neck and fingers, she was an accomplished pianist. She played the piano with her long fingers scrolling up and down the keys like she was gliding across water. I so look forward to seeing her again in heaven. She is no doubt worshiping and praising Jesus as I write this.

I can't remember how long it took me to work up the courage to pray out loud in the prayer group but it was months and months. Still, my heart and mind began to be renewed as I learned to sit in the presence of God week after week and heard those remarkable women worship, praise, repent, and pray. Witnessing this weekly taught me to do the same. I cherish those memories.

It was a tug-of-war battle learning to sit still. Part of conquering my flesh was to battle every kind of thought passing through my mind. I can remember pondering everything from grocery lists to what pretty shoes people had on in the prayer group, but the important thing was I was there. Can you believe there were times that I didn't want to go? By then, I had young kids around me all day -- not just mine, but I babysat five others - and I was tired. I am so very grateful to my mother-in-law who would pick me up every Tuesday, no matter what, she would come and I would be ready. I learned perseverance, to not give up but to follow through, whether I felt like it or not, rain or shine. I was in the Word of God daily and at prayer group every week. The best way I battled my own flesh and thoughts was through the practice of contemplative prayer. I'm so grateful.

Today, there is every kind of distraction to keep us from being still and our phones are one of the biggest ones. We have to be intentional about everything we put in our hands, hearts and minds in order to accomplish anything. The more I walk with Jesus the more I realize that I can't do anything without Him, nor would I want to. Still, in my flesh, sometimes I try. We are blessed to have a Savior who waits patiently for us. He is never in a rush but meets us exactly where we are. Now to sit for hours in His presence is not hard for me to do. It's a privilege and always a retreat. Daily times spent with Him are the most cherished moments of my life.

Jesus set this example for us over and over as He would go off alone to be with the Father. No way could He have loved us and accomplished the Cross if He hadn't. Let's not assume just because He was Jesus that life and time spent with the Father was easy. He had so much tugging on Him, so many looking to Him. Yet, He learned obedience and set time apart just as we are also told to do, and He did this long before His ministry began, so He was ready. The time Jesus spent with the Father equipped Him for every kind of trouble He would face; it steadied and readied Him.

I think often on the story of the storm in Mark 4:35-41. As the storm raged around them, the disciples panicked with fear, Jesus slept. I can't help but laugh at the thought. Can you imagine the deep sleep He must have been in? So deep that they had to wake him up? Then, as someone completely annoyed by the disturbance of His sleep, He yelled out, "Quiet! Be Still." Afterward, He asked the disciples, "Why are you so afraid? Don't you have faith?" I wish I could have been there but I'm sure I'd be panicked along with the disciples. How many of us can say that if a storm was raging violently around us, we could sleep? Some people really can. Why? Because they prepared ahead of time. They sat with the Lord enough that they knew Him, loved Him, and trusted Him. This is our "fire insurance," our greatest opportunity to prepare ahead of time.

"But seek first the kingdom of God and His righteousness, and all these things will be provided for you." – Matthew 6:33

This verse is telling us that we have no need to fear what is to come. As we seek Jesus, He will certainly take care of us even in our moment of death. To be still in His presence is to cross over into HIS realm; to walk by the Spirit is to allow His kingdom to come within us, and around us.

In the Stillness

4 – Worship, Praise, Thanksgiving

Worship the LORD your God, and his blessing will be on your food and water. I will take away sickness from among you. – Exodus 23:25

As I shared earlier, when I began my journey learning to pray, it all started with worship, praise, and thanksgiving. I can't express enough the importance of these expressions. Though they are different, they are similar as they work together.

Why these three? Worship is what the Lord is due.

"Ascribe to the LORD the glory due his name; worship the LORD in the splendor of his holiness." – Psalm 29:2

Worship – to worship is to express reverence and adoration of deity. In Hebrew it means to bend, prostrate oneself, adore, admire, revere, idolize. It may be to truly worship is to not have music at all but to be totally submitted to the Lord, prostrate before Him saying nothing, in reverence and awe of His greatness. Still, I can't imagine not having music.

To worship is to humble ourselves and acknowledge our need of God in our lives. It's acknowledging the true God, yielding to His spirit, allowing Him to flow through us, adoring Him the way

He wants to be and is so deserving of. Worship gives the Holy Spirit permission to work through us.

"God is spirit, and those who worship him must worship in spirit and in truth" – John 4:24.

To worship in spirit and truth paves the way into the Holy of Holies. Worship flows with thanksgiving and praise. Worship prepares our hearts for an encounter with God and expects one to happen.

Praise – to praise is to express a favorable judgment of; commend; to glorify especially by the attribution of perfections; to express praise.

 To praise the Lord is to say it, to bring forth the words of admiration in your hearts for Him - for who He is and for all that He has done.

"Enter His gates with thanksgiving and his courts with praise. Give thanks to Him, bless His name." – Psalm 100:4

The Temple of Jerusalem was surrounded by gates and courts. A veil (heavy curtain) covered the entrance into the Holy of Holies. As many know, when Jesus died the veil was torn, making it possible for any who wanted access to Him to enter into the Holy of Holies. However, Psalm 100:4 illustrates a journey in getting there. Being thankful is part of that journey.

Thankful – to be thankful is to be pleased and relieved, expressing gratitude and relief.

Though Jesus made the way to Himself accessible and open to us, He didn't automatically sit us down in the Holy of Holies. We have to enter in and go through the gates and the courts by giving Him thanks and praising Him, allowing truth by His spirit to start our steps. In this verse He is telling us what pleases Him. To thank Him is to acknowledge all that He has done for us and will do. Thankful hearts say, "We trust you Lord for what we can't see and for what is still to come." Thankfulness is a high form of trusting the Lord that pushes back the enemy's attacks that come through doubt and disbelief.

One time while we were on the mission field my son Micah was very sick. All night he made many trips to the bathroom with vomiting and diarrhea until he was dehydrated and couldn't walk anymore due to being so weak. I didn't know what to do. Micah was lethargic and barely talking. I carried him to the bathroom and sat him on the toilet. I prayed again asking the Lord what to do. The Holy Spirit said, "Praise Me." I told Micah what the Lord said and that little boy began praising the Lord with me, though he could barely talk. We sat there together telling the Lord how wonderful He was and praising Him for being so kind as to speak to us. It broke the sickness; Micah went right to bed and slept through the night. Some might say, "Why didn't God just stop it anyway?" I'd say He did, but through us. It was an attack, warfare against our family. Praising the Lord during that taught us that praise and worship will transcend our circumstance and the devil hates it. GOD IS FAITHFUL! (Exodus 23:25)

It's all about walking into a relationship with Him. He will not let us skip this journey of getting to Him. Why? Because it is in the journey where we find Him, know Him, and change into His likeness. It is in the journey that our real identity comes forth (Galatians 2:20).

In the Old Testament the worshipers and singers praising God always preceded the Ark of the Covenant. We see a divine order here, the worship and praise in front of an encounter with God, the righteous Ark of the Covenant. If you want the favor of God in your life, start worshipping and praising Him more. Nothing will get you to Him faster.

I can only imagine the unseen praise and worship that was happening at the birth of Christ. There is no doubt in my mind that a symphony of music from the heavens accompanied His arrival as the angels announced it. He is a God of Praise!

> "Praise the LORD!
> Praise the LORD from the heavens;
> Praise Him in the heights!
> Praise Him, all His angels;

Praise Him, all His hosts!

Praise Him, sun and moon;

Praise Him, all the stars of light!

Praise Him, highest heavens,

And the waters above the heavens!

They are to praise the name of the LORD,

For He commanded and they were created.

He has also established them forever and ever;

He has made a decree and it will not pass away."

– Psalm 148:1-6

I believe there is no quicker way to our Father's heart than through worship and praising Him. I also believe it is the most powerful form of warfare. Worship and praise can break the bondage of sickness and the attacks of the devil, ushering in humility and acknowledging our need of the Lord. When you don't know what else to do, stop to worship and praise God.

Another time when our family was on the mission field in the Philippines, we were living at an orphanage and an adjacent field caught on fire. In America if you have a fire you call 9-1-1, and fire trucks come in a few minutes. In the Philippines, there were few to go around and they could take hours to get to you. The fire was headed towards the orphanage, so we and our team stood outside facing the fire and began to worship, sing, and praise the Lord. It first broke our fear, so we began to intercede and pray for the Lord to come to put the fire out. We did our part and laid the ground work for the Lord to come and do His, and boy did He. It was a clear day with no clouds, but as we prayed, we watched a rain cloud come directly over the fire in the field. We continued to watch as the rain poured on the fire until it was out. True story. Nothing is impossible for Jesus if we trust and believe Him.

How did we know to do that? By the prompting of the Holy Spirit, we saw God move. He speaks and urges us into the direction that will bring Him the most glory. This teaches us to not second guess what we sense Him telling us to do, leading us into safety. Do you think our faith was encouraged that day? You bet it was! Do you think these kinds of miracles can become normal in our lives? Jesus longs for them to. He is so amazing.

5 – The Beauty of Repentance

"I tell you that in the same way, there will be more joy in heaven over one sinner who repents than over ninety-nine righteous people who have no need of repentance."
– Luke 15:7

I guess when one thinks of something beautiful, repentance is not the first thing that comes to mind. I see repentance as beautiful because of what it accomplishes for us. To be able to repent to the Lord and to others in our lives is one of life's greatest gifts. It is definitely not a natural thing but another action that needs to be practiced.

In the power of repentance comes our true salvation. To repent we must surrender our control, our independence, our will, and the biggest, our pride, laying these down and calling out to the only One who can save us and bring us close to His heart.

"For thus the Lord GOD, the Holy One of Israel, has said, 'In repentance and rest you will be saved; in quietness and trust is your strength.' But you were not willing." – Isaiah 30:15

"But you were not willing." Look at what the Lord is saying. To be saved means SOZO, to have salvation, healing, to be born again and more. We have a *choice* to repent and rest in our salvation.

"Therefore repent and return, so that your sins may be wiped away, in order that times of refreshing may come from the presence of the Lord." – Acts 3:19

This verse tells us that we are far from the Lord when we have sin in our lives, that repentance brings us back to Him, and that His presence will bring us a refreshing season in our relationship with Him, wiping our sins completely away. God is so good. This may not be new revelation for you but it is by hearing again and again that our faith is renewed. Jesus promised to never leave us nor forsake us, so when there is distance between us and Him it is always our doing. Even if He uses the distance for our training and good, it is still our doing.

To repent is also to walk into a healthy fear of the Lord, which is the beginning of wisdom.

"The fear of the LORD is the beginning of wisdom, and the knowledge of the Holy One is understanding." – Proverbs 9:10

(By the way, anytime you see LORD in the Bible it means you are reading about God the Father and the Son together, He is emphasizing this when you see His name in capital letters).

The fear of the LORD tells our spirit man that if we don't repent there will be consequences to our actions. A life of daily repentance keeps our hearts and minds in check, clean and without anything to block our relationship with Him. It puts our pride in its place and reminds us that we need God and others in our lives.

John the Baptist tells us that we can't bear fruit without repentance.

"Therefore bear fruit in keeping with repentance; and do not suppose that you can say to yourselves, "We have Abraham for our father," for I say to you that from these stones God is able to raise up children to Abraham. The axe is already laid at the root of the trees; therefore every tree that does not bear good fruit is cut down and thrown into the fire." – Matthew 3:8-10

This coincides with John 15. Jesus explains that if we are not bearing fruit, then we are not His disciples. Therefore, if we are not living a life of repentance so that we can bear fruit, neither can we be His disciples.

Lack of repentance will justify every kind of sin that's active in our life and in our past, allowing a double mindedness to set in. This will feed our pride, telling us that we don't need to repent -- that it will work itself out. It is a lie and a trap. To ignore sin is to feed it!

"Come close to God and He come close to you. Cleanse your hands, you sinners; and purify your hearts, you double-minded." – James 4:8

Without the daily work of "cleansing" through repentance, our mind will be in chaos, not knowing who we are nor what we are to do, and will be without peace. Double mindedness is a miserable state of being and we've all been there.

There is a catch to repentance though. Real repentance means that we will not repeat the sin. The slate is not only clean on God's side as He has forgiven us, but we are saying we will not stay on that path of sin. If we return to the same sin over and over, we become double-minded, as I've shared before, and it gets harder and harder to begin again.

"If we confess our sins, He is faithful and righteous, so that He will forgive us our sins and cleanse us from all unrighteousness. If we say that we have not sinned, we make Him a liar and His word is not in us." – 1 John 1:9-10

So, if we don't acknowledge our sin, we are calling God a liar and His word is not living and active in us by His Holy Spirit. Yikes! Feel the fear of the Lord in that? I sure do. We are basically saying that He is not who He says He is and we, as His children, are not capable of overcoming sin. If we are not acknowledging our sin, then the Cross was for nothing.

Sometimes we continue to sin with the same issues. This tells us we are striving in our own flesh and not in the power of what Jesus has provided for us. This is not to bring condemnation on anyone but for us to realize the Lord has provided a higher way for us. He made us capable through the Cross. Yay Jesus!!!

"I can do all things through Him who strengthens me." – Philippians 4:13

It is never by ourselves that we can accomplish something righteous. It's always about Jesus and His accomplishments through us. Of course, people can overcome things all the time without the Lord, but all it accomplishes is to breed an independent spirit that doesn't need God. It is a terrible trap of the devil to be so independent. Women have become masters at this in our quest for equality with men, but that's another book.

Here is a story to illustrate this point. Years ago I had an addiction to sugar. I was a "closet eater," secretly devouring cupcakes, Little Debbie's, and ice cream at every opportunity. I was careful what I fed my kids but I had my secret stashes where I would go and binge eat sugary yumminess. Perhaps some of you can relate.

One day the Holy Spirit said to me while I was in my quiet time, "Caron, if you don't stop eating sugar you will be taking insulin." It was that clear. Later that day I told my husband what the Lord had said to me. I cried for a week. I knew that I had been in sin and that I had to stop. I had made sugar a god in my life and I had to have it daily. I repented to the Lord for this. My husband Mike was so precious to stop eating sugar with me. I did a 6-

month sugar fast... NO sugar! It was hard. I had sugar withdrawal so bad that I stained my side of the mattress by sweating through our new burgundy sheets! I even called a Hotline for help and was told I was having severe sugar withdrawal, similar to the withdrawal from a drug addiction. We know now from more studies that sugar has the same effect in the brain as using cocaine does. Still, I kept at it out of obedience to the Lord and my sugar addiction broke! By His grace the consequences of sickness associated with it broke, too. No insulin!

The Lord is so good that through our repentance He might even stop our consequences. Not always, but I do believe most of the time He does, as He is so merciful. To this day I live a lifestyle with little to no sugar. I for sure have seasons but I can stop eating sugar whenever the Lord tells me to, or if I'm doing a fast. It no longer has a hold on me. I am confident I could not have done it without Him. How I thank Him!

"Whatever you do, do your work heartily as for the Lord rather than for men, knowing that from the Lord you will receive the reward of the inheritance. It is the Lord Christ whom you serve." – Colossians 3:23-24

To live in the flesh has no reward but whatever we do, if we do it for Jesus, we get a reward for it. We need a new outlook on all of our daily work! Obedience comes with a reward. Praise be to Him whose arms are always ready to forgive and receive us.

"As far as the east is from the west, so far has He removed our transgressions from us." – Psalm 103:12

Jesus will not turn a sincere heart away. Never. He is so loving and faithful. The closer our relationship is to Jesus, the more we want to please Him and live a lifestyle of daily repentance and renewal. Our choices to repent reflect the closeness of our relationship to Him and to others.

In the Stillness

6 – Forgiveness

As far as the east is from the west, so far has He removed our wrongdoings from us. – Psalm 103:12

Repentance sparks the action of forgiveness. Without forgiveness there would be no restart or clean slate. The holy setup of Jesus coming to earth was for our forgiveness of sins and eternal life. What a good God we have.

God has so beautifully paved the way to show us what true forgiveness looks like through His Son. Jesus paid it all, took it all upon Himself, thus enabling us to forgive others. There is *no sin* that He did not die for. We just have to repent and receive His amazing forgiveness.

"…Repent and be baptized, every one of you, in the name of Jesus Christ for the forgiveness of your sins. And you will receive the gift of the Holy Spirit." – Acts 2:38

For some people, forgiveness can be an immediate thing. For most, however, the choice to forgive must take place over and over in the heart as the enemy repeatedly brings to mind the hurts and offenses of the past.

"Then Peter came and said to Him 'Lord, how often shall my brother sin against me and I forgive him? Up to seven times?'

Jesus said to him, 'I do not say to you, up to seven times, but up to seventy times seven.'" – Matthew 18:21-22

This tells us that we don't give up on loving or forgiving people. But just to add, we can forgive someone and still need to separate ourselves from them. There are seasons for relationships and sometimes they come to an end. There is nothing wrong with that. Of course, if we are dealing with family members it is another story that may require us to deal with matters in a long-suffering way.

Forgiveness is a command and we are told to do it just as Jesus himself did. If we are to be like Christ, we mustn't neglect this part.

"Be kind to one another, compassionate, forgiving each other, just as God in Christ also has forgiven you." – Ephesians 4:32

To forgive is to acknowledge the blood sacrifice of Jesus for our sins, and for the sins of others. It is the redeeming power of His grace that has freed us from all bondage of sin. As we forgive others, we are freeing ourselves from condemnation and enabling ourselves to love others as Jesus loved.

"In him we have redemption through his blood, the forgiveness of sins, in accordance with the riches of God's grace." – Ephesians 1:7

Sometimes we may question if we have *really* forgiven someone, when guilt or a memory creeps back up provoking bad feelings. As we confess forgiveness with our mouth and hear it with our ears, we can trust that the spoken words of our mouth are true and real, even if it takes time for the heart and mind to catch up with it. Forgiveness and repentance go hand in hand in this way. This is part of working out our obedience (see Philippians 2:12). We continue to forgive as long as is necessary, until lasting forgiveness takes root in our hearts and minds. To forgive is to be obedient to Jesus.

I remember I once had to forgive someone that had done me wrong my entire life. I was so hurt and angry. I cried out to the Lord, asking Him to show me this person as He saw them. I immediately saw them as a child, a wounded child that did not get the nurturing they needed. I cried for hours over what the Holy Spirit was showing me. I had also seen ALL that this person had said and done towards me and at the end of my crying I had forgiven them completely. It was totally God, as my heart was filled with such love for them and understanding of the wounded person they were. No memory ever had a sting after that. I was able to love them as Jesus loves them.

I heard God that day: His heart, the memories he took me through, His spiritual voice and direction, and the ability to forgive. It was all because He wanted me free of the deep wounds in my heart, but it wasn't until I cried out to Him to show me the way to forgive, to show me the person as He saw them.

How merciful the Lord is. He will do this for you, too, if you only ask Him. Hallelujah!

As I shared, forgiveness not only frees us up but it is what the Lord has commanded of us if we too want His forgiveness. It's part of our obedience and love towards Him and others.

"For if you forgive other people for their offenses, your heavenly Father will also forgive you. But if you do not forgive other people, then your Father will not forgive your offenses."
– Matthew 6:14-15

In their anger and pride, I've seen many people harbor unforgiveness, and it trickles into every area of their lives. Unforgiveness is a prison that never allows us to fully be at peace or rest. People become bitter, angry, and miserable. I'm sure we all know people like this, who surely have unforgiveness in their hearts.

Unforgiveness can also play a role in our sicknesses. As we harbor offenses and hurts, it eats away at our soul, our mind and body, eventually manifesting in illnesses. Of course, not all illness stems from unforgiveness, but I think we'd be surprised at how much of it does. It also keeps us from being righteous before the Lord, as we are in disobedience.

"Therefore, confess your sins to one another, and pray for one another so that you may be healed. A prayer of a righteous person, when it is brought about, can accomplish much." – James 5:16

Could it be so simple to say that the world is in the shape that it's in because God's children have not forgiven one another, repented, and received forgiveness from Jesus? I believe the responsibility lies with us.

"If my people, which are called by my name, shall humble themselves, and pray, and seek my face, and turn from their wicked ways; then I will hear from heaven, and will forgive their sin, and will heal their land." – 2 Chronicles 7:14

I believe it is as simple as this verse. The key here is to humble ourselves, telling the Lord that we need Him. God knows our hearts; He knows if we are sincere or not. He also knows our deep wounds and why we do what we do. He is certainly long-suffering and merciful toward us. He looks for our humility and desire to be righteous as He is righteous. He does not look for our perfection; He looks for our willingness. Praise Him.

7 – Contemplative Prayer

I will meditate on Your precepts and regard Your ways.
– Psalm 119:15

[Lectio Divina & getting started]

After worship, praise, thanksgiving, and any repentance, we can certainly petition the Lord for our needs and wants in full confidence that He will answer us. It's not that the Lord won't hear us if we don't do this, it's that He too has a way that He wants to be approached, just as we do. And yes, it's not just about our needs. He certainly cares about our wants, too.

"So if you, despite being evil, know how to give good gifts to your children, how much more will your Father who is in heaven give good things to those who ask Him." – Matthew 7:11

 We are told to come boldly and with confidence to the throne of grace (Hebrews 4:16). The Lord cares about every aspect of our lives and longs to have us ask Him, petition Him, interceding on behalf of ourselves, others, and our world. As I've shared, contemplative prayer and Lectio Divina is where I began my journey. Contemplative prayer is praying with our hearts and minds, in a meditative manner. Lectio Divina adds a bit more. This style of praying is what brought me into the deep presence of God through the written Word. What began as a learned habit became automatic and natural. Of course, there are many ways to pray. This was just my starting point. For those who already have an active prayer life, maybe this will bring something new for a season. If we are open, there is no end to what we can learn from the Holy Spirit.

Lectio Divina was started by the Monastic Monks in 1500 AD. The Monks were taught to read and contemplate God's Word, sometimes spending months on one verse. They would go before the Lord with the verse they were led to read and allow their senses to be a part of their prayer. Being still as they pondered the verse, they would reflect and chew on every word: How does that verse or word sound, smell, taste, and look before the Lord? What would the Holy Spirit want to say to me through that verse? The Monks were taught that while they were doing their daily chores, if any thought or scripture entered their minds they were to stop and meditate on it. Using their senses, they would ponder God's Word and wait for Him to minister to them. It's a powerful way to commune with God and it changed my life.

I'm not teaching Catholicism or any one denomination. Back when the Monks practiced this meditation, Bibles were not readily available. Monks would gather together for readings and ponder the scriptures. It was a way to make the Word last, spread it out, and go deep. If I've learned anything from being in missions, it's that Jesus can teach us something through anyone and any circumstance. We can certainly learn from the Monks and their dedication to Christ. We will find pieces of Him in all religions; of course, all religions do not lead us to salvation. Jesus said,

"I am the truth and the way, NO ONE comes to the Father but through me." – John 14:6

Jesus is sneaky; I call him "Sneaky Jehovah" because He finds a way to infiltrate everything! He is in all religions. If we can find a root of truth, we can share the Gospel out of that root with those that are lost. Jesus finds a way to plant seeds whenever we are open to what and how He wants to speak, but it must line up with His Word. The Word of God must be our foundation for our growth and all that we share with others.

Outside of the prayer group I attended, I began practicing prayer at home. My first real touch from God as an adult came when I was 19 and newly married. I was sitting on the floor in our apartment praying when a beam of sunlight came through the window and fell right on me. No words were spoken but it was a powerful moment for me as I knew the presence of the Lord was there. The warmth was more than just a sunbeam; it permeated my whole being. I sat there with the Lord and allowed Him to radiate His love throughout my body. It was my first personal experience in the Spirit that crossed over into the natural.

Over the next two years I would continue attending the prayer group until my husband got transferred with his job to Omaha, Nebraska. There, I spent much time in prayer and the Holy Spirit took me to valleys and mountains, and to more valleys. It was a bittersweet time that I wouldn't trade for anything.

I faced many things with the Lord in those valley experiences. He showed me things about myself, wounds from my past, words spoken over me that I had allowed to take root. He began to show me how to allow Him to heal me. I say *allow* because many times we think that we are going to have an instantaneous soul healing as we pray for it. Actually, Jesus did this on the Cross; through His death, He gave all that was needed for our healing, but we still have to walk it out.

"by his stripes (or scourging) we are healed" – Isaiah 53:5

I believe this to be true but we have to allow Him into our hearts and minds to truly heal us. We can have salvation but if we don't embrace the whole of the Word and the personhood of Jesus we can still suffer from sickness and disease; this is what the devil desires for us. There is nothing that can't be accomplished through faith in who Jesus is and what He did for us on the Cross. Many people don't want to hear this. Do I believe every circumstance is like this? No. Just as the devil was given permission to sift Job, so there are seasons for us as well.

When we are saved, we are SOZO. The Greek word "sozo" means salvation, delivered, complete, and healed. When we become saved, but we don't walk out our total salvation, it is not His doing but our own circumstances blocking the way. There is no judgment in that statement, it just means the problems are within and all around us.

I once heard a pastor say that his little 3-year-old son died of leukemia and that it was God's will and his son's "time" to go to heaven. Let me be very clear here, it is *never* God's will that we die of sickness and disease. If this were true, Jesus' death was for nothing. This doesn't mean that God won't use a person's death and circumstance, regardless of what happened, to teach us or to glorify Himself. Jesus can use anything. Jesus came to conquer death, He is the God of LIFE, not death. If we say it's His will for us to die of sickness and disease, then it's like we are comparing Him to Allah who *wills* death. It is a lie from the pit of hell! Even as I write this, my dander is up -- I am so passionate about this matter! Regardless of how a person dies, we can have peace if a Christian dies from sickness or disease, knowing they will be with Jesus in heaven and healed on the other side.

"...but now has been revealed by the appearing of our Savior Christ Jesus, who abolished death and brought life and immortality to light through the gospel." – 2 Timothy 1:10

You might ask why so many Christians are dying from illnesses. There are a few reasons: 1) unbelief and lack of faith; 2) lifestyles of carelessness and sin; 3) warfare with a real enemy that attacks our bodies. But the third is still attached to the first two. It never stands alone, since Jesus has given us all we need to defeat the devil.

The problem never comes from Heaven but is always here on earth. Whether it lies in the lack of faith, lack of knowledge, poor care of our bodies, or attacks of the enemy, it is never the will of God. There is no condemnation in these statements. We have to believe and take the stance that Jesus finished the work on the cross and by His stripes we were truly healed, SOZO! If we allow our mind to accept anything else then our entire faith system will be rocked. Truly it will. We must *know* that Jesus equipped us for everything through the cross. Yet, He will not make us believe this. It is our job to be in the Word, be in His presence and walk out our salvation and healing.

I've dealt with sickness my whole life. Knowing the truth of God's Word and His heart, yet still dealing with sickness has been very hard for me. Yet, I refuse to allow my circumstance to dictate a false character of Christ to me. I know without a doubt it's always His will to heal me. I must choose Him, choose His truths, and never give up.

Jesus is such a gentleman. He will never force himself on us. Jesus did many miracles but most of them were "Go and be healed." We have to partner with Him on a daily basis and give Him permission to enter all areas of our hearts and minds. We can receive salvation, but many of us block the possession of the whole word "Sozo." Through Sozo Jesus is living and active in our lives. He is the WORD in our flesh. Through His fullness, wholeness, and grace is the truth made known to us (John 1:14-18). Thanks be to God.

> "But He was pierced through for our transgressions,
> He was crushed for our iniquities;
> the chastening for our well-being fell upon Him,
> And by His scourging we are healed.
> All of us like sheep have gone astray,
> Each of us has turned to his own way;
> But the Lord has caused the iniquity of us all
> To fall on Him." – Isaiah 53:5-6

"And He Himself bore our sins in His body on the cross, so that we might die to sin and live to righteousness; for by His wounds you were healed." – 1 Peter 2:24

This is truly amazing. Everything that we could possibly go through in life, Jesus took care of on the Cross. He gave us our real identity as Christians, sons and daughters of the Most High

King. He gave us the ability to live whole and righteous lives with His healing and power.

When God looks at us He sees His finished work on the Cross that made us complete through Him. He already bore our sickness and shame so He will not see it any longer when He looks upon us. He made a way for our new life! As He promised to never leave us nor forsake us, He can only do this by seeing us as His finished work on the Cross. After we become a believer, the only way to be separated from the Lord is if we choose to walk away. Still, He is always waiting on us to call upon His name and draw us near to Him. Hallelujah!

Some of what I have shared in this chapter will be hard for some to receive. I understand that, but I challenge all of us to dig deep into the Word for ourselves and ask Jesus to reveal His truths about His heart when it comes to healing.

8 – Practice Daily Life in the Word

For the word of God is living and active, sharper than any two-edged sword, piercing to the division of soul and of spirit, of joints and of marrow, and discerning the thoughts and intentions of the heart. – Hebrew 4:12

We moved back to Kentucky after we had 2 of our 3 sons in Omaha, Nebraska. I began attending Margaret's prayer group again and going deeper into a prayer life with God. It was so good to be back among such godly women of prayer.

I read, prayed and watched kids all at the same time every day. I read so many books, sometimes two a week. I was a sponge soaking up all that I could. I just wanted more and more of Jesus. I still today truly love to read about Him.

Reading was always difficult for me, due to dyslexia. I didn't really take off reading until late in my teens and still didn't know what was "wrong" with me. It was my prayer life that healed me of my insecurities of reading. I later learned from the Lord that my dyslexia was actually related to my gifts and calling. So sad that we are quick to label people. We are all so beautifully made and what the Lord sees as His workmanship, sometimes the world will see as defects. Still, Jesus can fix how the world damages us through labels as we follow after Him.

"But seek first His kingdom and His righteousness, and all these things will be added to you." – Matthew 6:33

I love how the Lord will always answer our heart's desire for more of Him. Even if we have to wait a while, He *always* answers.

To learn to sit in the presence of Jesus meant that I had to be very intentional. I had a set time every day in the mornings to be in the Word and wait on the Holy Spirit to speak to me. Daily for one hour, I taught my little boys to play quietly or watch their shows and to only disturb Momma if they really needed something. The Holy Spirit can also speak to kids in such a beautiful way. They understand so much more than we realize. The kids were usually very good and of course my door was always open. We had a small home and it was my time with the Lord that would set the tone for the entire day. Of course, I was within feet of my children while spending time with Jesus and they were never unattended.

It was during these years when I began to realize how deeply the Lord wants to commune with us, His children. He longs to be with us and show us unique things that are just between us and Him. His Word tells us:

"No eye has seen no ear has heard no mind has conceived what God has prepared for those who love him -- but God has revealed it to us by his Spirit. The Spirit searches all things, even the deep things of God." – 1 Corinthians 2:6-10

Life is still the same, in that I continue to be intentional about spending time with the Lord. But what's different is I now have an abiding presence with Him. Over the years, my relationship with Him has grown to a place where sitting down and reading the Word is a continuation of my routine with Him, waking up and speaking with Him, sometimes acknowledging His presence without saying anything at all but just *being* with Him. To practice daily life with Jesus is to include Him on all that we do. That might sound eccentric to some, but it's truly supposed to be our normal way of living.

Being a student of the Word is quite different than just reading the Bible. To study, to truly be educated by the Word of God, is the highest education we can ever work to achieve. There is no degree on earth that can compare to learning and hiding the Word within our heart. It is not only our weapon of warfare but it is our very food for survival and eternal salvation. HE is the Word within us. Of course, we can find all the knowledge we desire in the Word, but without relationship it is absent of the very thing that makes it meaningful, the guidance of His precious Holy Spirit.

"And the Word became flesh, and dwelt among us; and we saw His glory, glory as of the only Son from the Father, full of grace and truth." – John 1:14

As we receive Jesus, we also receive His glory. We are His true crown and His glory, His Bride that He awaits patiently. We have to come to the realization that Jesus loves us so much, He has imparted Himself to us. When He looks at us, filled with His Spirit, He truly does see Himself. When we grasp this reality, there is nothing that can stop us from doing the kingdom's work.

Protect, through the Holy Spirit who dwells in us, the treasure which has been entrusted to you.
– 2 Timothy 1:14

When I share about contemplative prayer using Lectio Divina and its origins, I realize that the Monks did the best they could to explain what would happen if we would sit in the presence of the Lord, dissecting His Word, chewing on it and allowing Him to reveal Himself to us through Scripture. I don't think anyone can do the Lord justice trying to explain the incredible things He chooses to show us when we dedicate ourselves to His presence daily.

Contemplate is defined: To look thoughtfully for a long time at. Think about. Think profoundly and at length; meditate. This word "contemplate" gives the Holy Spirit room to reveal Himself however He wants. As we look upon Him, His word, and wait for Him to speak, He gets to come to us in the way that He wishes.

Lectio Divina – "The Divine Reading," has five main steps: Be Silent, Read, Contemplate, Pray and Rest.

I don't want to dive too deep into the practice of Lectio Divina, since this is a tool only and can never make up for the spontaneity of the Holy Spirit. As I began this journey as a student (we are always students), I learned that the Holy Spirit had His own unique way of speaking to me just as He does with everyone. No need to get jealous or sad with what someone else has in a relationship with the Lord. If you put your time in with Him, He will meet you in a unique and beautiful way.

In the practice of Lectio Divina, you submit your whole being to Jesus. Use all of your senses and your whole self to love Jesus. This can be practiced as individuals or corporately. Begin by:

1) BE SILENT – Begin your time of meditating on God's Word in silence. Calm yourself and thoughts focusing on God's will.

2) READ – Choose a passage of scripture reading it out loud slowly. Imagine the passage. Use all of your senses, asking the Lord to show you, "How does this passage Look, Sound, Feel, Taste and Smell?" What does the Scripture say that is obvious to me, the reader?

3) CONTEMPLATE, REFLECT OR MEDITATE – Read the passage again, chewing on every word, understanding what each means. Capture every thought, asking the Lord how it relates to the passage. How does the Scripture relate to me and what is going on in my life?

4) RESPOND IN PRAYER – Pray. Enter into dialog with the Holy Spirit. Be honest, expressing any emotions of joy, anger or even grief. Pray and express to the Lord what is on your heart concerning the Scripture.

5) REST – What is the Lord saying to me about this Scripture through my mind, heart, soul and strength? Receive what the Holy Spirit is saying to you. Let go of your own ideas and thoughts. Listen deeply to the still, small voice of God. Allow yourself and Holy Spirit to flow together receiving His truth. Embrace moments where words are not necessary, just soaking in the presence of Jesus.

Allow your senses and mind to be *in* the Word with Jesus. Let Him guide your imagination. Not a vain imagination, but a submitted heart and mind to the Holy Spirit's will. How does this Scripture sound, look, feel, smell and taste? There is no particular order here, just be in the Word and allow the Holy Spirit to come.

Just as John is so detailed in describing what he experienced in Revelation, so we too can also have an experience with the Holy Spirit. I understand that John had a mission to scribe and share with us all but it tells us that as children of God we have every right to meet Jesus, see His face and experience precious times with Him. As we read and meditate on the Word of God it can come alive within us.

As I have shared before, it can take time and practice to quiet one's mind to allow the Holy Spirit to have His way through us but He will certainly show up in a powerful way if we just give ourselves to Him. Just as 2 Timothy 1:14 says, He is a treasure within us!

Practice time! Take some time now to sit with the Lord and apply contemplative prayer through Lectio Divina. Find a quiet place and a Scripture verse and invite Him to come. If your mind begins to wonder, pull it back. Sometimes I send all the things that are coming at me in a bubble up to heaven for the Lord to deal with. This visual might help you to focus. Pull your mind and heart back to Him as many times as you need to do. I promise, He will not disappoint you.

10 – The Mind of Christ

With some of the stuff I've shared so far, maybe you are thinking, "This sounds a little strange, a little New Age."

One of the biggest injustices among Christians, besides the robbery of our Jewish heritage in Jesus, is the New Age movement. We've allowed it to scare us so much that we've thrown out the "mysteries of heaven" that rightfully belong to us. The New Age beliefs have mixed many religions together, but instead of taking the meat off the bone and throwing the rest away, we've declared it all wrong and robbed ourselves of much in the Spirit that belongs to Jesus. We've allowed this to happen because we don't know who we really are.

Most Christians are in an identity crisis and have no idea what it means to become a new creature in Christ. We are all on a journey, and continually changing, and going deeper in our relationship with Him. In His presence we find our true identity.

"Therefore, if anyone is in Christ, he is a new creation; the old things passed away; behold, new things have come." – 2 Corinthians 5:17

So how are we new creatures in Christ? Let's look at all of 1 Corinthians 2. As we read this together, I will comment throughout...

"[1] And when I came to you, brothers and sisters, I did not come as someone superior in speaking ability or wisdom, as I proclaimed to you the testimony of God. [2] For I determined to know nothing among you except Jesus Christ, and Him crucified. [3] I also was with you in weakness and fear, and in great trembling, [4] and my message and my preaching were not in persuasive words of wisdom, but in demonstration of the Spirit and of power, [5] so that your faith would not rest on the wisdom of mankind, but on the power of God."

Here Paul is saying that it is only by the power of the Spirit that he speaks and shares, not through words but out of his demonstration of the Spirit through him. Paul was a pretty smart man, a Pharisee lawyer and well-schooled. For Paul to tell us that he knows nothing, he's actually telling us that we are all on equal ground when it comes to being taught by the Spirit of the Lord.

"[6]Yet we do speak wisdom among those who are mature; a wisdom, however, not of this age nor of the rulers of this age, who are passing away; [7] but we speak God's wisdom in a mystery, the hidden wisdom which God predestined before the ages to our glory;"

The wisdom Paul is referring to has never been known before, nor has it been taught; it is fresh and new and still foreign. Few had the Holy Spirit to reveal truth to them. It was wisdom spoken before the earth was even formed but made known to all of us!

> "8 the wisdom which none of the rulers of this age has understood; for if they had understood it, they would not have crucified the Lord of glory; 9 but just as it is written:
> 'THINGS WHICH EYE HAS NOT SEEN AND EAR HAS NOT HEARD,
> AND WHICH HAVE NOT ENTERED THE HUMAN HEART,
> ALL THAT GOD HAS PREPARED FOR THOSE WHO LOVE HIM.'
>
> 10 For to us God revealed them through the Spirit; for the Spirit searches all things, even the depths of God."

In the Old Testament it was impossible to know the deep things of God as His Spirit had not been given to us yet. Even Noah, Abraham, Moses, David, etc. did not have what we are privileged to have now. Of course, they had the Word of God, but they were bound by the interpretation of God's personhood through the Law only, or if God showed up to speak to them through His Spirit, fire, smoke, or angels. It was not an indwelling presence like we have.

> "[11]For who among men knows the thoughts of a man,
> except the spirit of the man which is in him? Even so
> the thoughts of God no one knows except the Spirit of
> God. [12]Now we have received, not the spirit of the
> world, but the Spirit who is from God, so that we may
> know the things freely given to us by God, [13] which
> things we also speak, not in words taught by human
> wisdom, but in those taught by the Spirit, combining
> spiritual thoughts with spiritual words."

This is so exciting! It's clearly saying that because we have the
Spirit of God within us, we too can know the thoughts of God
by His Spirit that is freely given. He works through our own
thoughts directed by His Spirit. Isn't that a miracle?? We can
have the thoughts of God, the Creator of the universe!

> "[14]But a natural man does not accept the things of the
> Spirit of God, for they are foolishness to him; and he
> cannot understand them, because they are
> spiritually appraised."

This explains a lot about the world, doesn't it? It tells us those
who are not saved cannot possibly accept the things of the
Spirit of God; they think it is foolishness because there is no
understanding. Real spiritual understanding can only come
from the Holy Spirit interpreting it to us. I pray this helps us to

have more compassion on those we know who are not yet saved.

> "15But he who is spiritual appraises all things, yet he himself is appraised by no one."

We have the ability by the Spirit to appraise all things -- their value, significance, and worth -- but only God can appraise us; no other man can know our value or worth. How could they? We are co-heirs to the throne of God, sons and daughters of the Most High King. Few can grasp this meaning.

> "16FOR WHO HAS KNOWN THE MIND OF THE LORD, THAT HE WILL INSTRUCT HIM? But we have the mind of Christ."

Here are a few more definitions for fun that go along with this chapter:

Know – (Hebrew) **Yada** – to know in great variety of senses, figuratively, literally, experience, understand.

Love – (Greek) **agape** – to love in a social sense, dear, friend

Heart – (Greek) **kardia** (kardee-ah) – the thoughts, feelings, mind, also the middle (Hebrew) – the feelings, the will, intellect, mind understanding, wisdom.

Soul – (Greek) **Psuche** (psoo-khay') – Breath, heart, life, mind, soul, us.

Mind – (Greek) **dianoia** (dee-an-oy-ah) – deep thought, exercise, imagination, understanding, mind, know.

Strength – (Greek) **ischus** (is-khoos') – ability, might, power, strength

> The Old Testament says;

> "You shall love the LORD your God with all your heart and with all your soul and with all your strength." – Deuteronomy 6:5

> The New Testament says;

> "And He said to him, "You shall love the Lord your God with all your heart, and with all your soul, and with all your mind." – Matthew 22:37

We see the difference between the verses. The ability to love the Lord with our MIND had not yet been made available. The previous definitions show us that in the definitions of *love, heart,* and *mind,* they ALL have "mind" as a part of their definition. When *mind* was added, it adds imagination too because of the Holy Spirit and His capabilities. This is amazing!

They were only able to love the Lord in the Old Testament in the soulish mind (that which is of the written Law) and in might (the fleshly strength, rather than spiritual).

Our soul houses our mind, our will and our emotions. In the Old Testament their minds were not able to be made new yet.

Jesus had to do this for us on the Cross and give us His Holy Spirit.

When we get to the New Testament, Jesus prophesies by telling them to love the Lord God with "all of your heart, soul, and *mind*," even when He knew they couldn't yet. Jesus knew that His time was short and that the Spirit would soon be there to dwell within their minds and hearts.

The Holy Spirit lives within our conscience and though the heart is connected, it is the mind and Spirit that direct us. We can see the words in common in the previous definitions with the heart, soul, and mind.

"For our proud confidence is this: the testimony of our conscience, that in holiness and godly sincerity, not in fleshly wisdom but in the grace of God, we have conducted ourselves in the world, and especially toward you." – 2 Corinthians 1:12

Now we can see just how lost people are without the Holy Spirit in their lives -- how a mind without the Spirit of the Lord is subject to anything. Their fleshly desires, and the devil who directs their thoughts, fill them with fear at every opportunity without the possibility of real freedom. They are ruled by their flesh, their own thoughts, their will and emotions. Having the Holy Spirit means we have the ability to have real peace and rest from ourselves.

When our minds are submitted to the Holy Spirit, He can truly show us anything He wants. He can give us His vision and take us many places in the Spirit with Him.

If you look at these definitions you see how they overlap one another and are connected. To know and love the Lord is to know Him in a variety of senses and in a social way, with your heart, soul, mind and strength. It is all interconnected with the mind and imagination.

To love Him with our strength was no longer in the Old Testament physical sense but with our minds in the courageous sense, steadfast, powerful and by the Spirit. Of course, I know some godly *Power Lifters* that truly love the Lord in their physical strength, but they would agree their abilities would be meaningless without the Spirit of the Lord.

"'Not by might nor by power, but by My Spirit,' says the LORD of hosts." – Zechariah 4:6

This verse was the prophetic word spoken through Zerubbabel, speaking of things to come.

To be strong is to house the steadfast peace of God within our hearts and minds, trusting Him to guide, speak and direct us.

"The steadfast of mind You will keep in perfect peace, because he trusts in You." – Isaiah 26:3

What an amazing God we serve!

Now we can see why the devil robbed us through the New Age movement and wanted to scare us off. He knows that a mind submitted to the Holy Spirit is a *powerful* one that houses our real identity in Jesus. We would be unstoppable for the Kingdom if we could step into who we really are.

In the Stillness

11 – Imagination

"We are destroying speculations and every lofty thing raised up against the knowledge of God, and we are taking every thought captive to the obedience of Christ,"
– 2 Corinthians 10:5

In some translations, the Word talks about having "vain" imaginations. I like the NASB, as it's close to the original language and words it a bit differently.

This describes the war around and within us, the war against our own flesh to "take every thought captive." The biggest battle we deal with as Christians is the battle of the mind: self-doubt, fear, and evil thoughts that can torment us in our imaginations. They're all at war against the Spirit of God within us. However, a mind submitted to the Holy Spirit allows *Him* to dictate where our mind goes. Meeting Him there within the imagination and through the Word of God is the most powerful force within us. Paul continues…

"You are looking at things as they are outwardly. If anyone is confident in himself that he is Christ's, let him consider this again within himself, that just as he is Christ's, so also are we."
– 2 Corinthians 10:7

Paul is not saying to look within yourself for your own capabilities. He is clearly saying that as we belong to Christ, so He lives within us, and it is there where we can choose to reside alongside of Him. We can practice allowing Him to take over so that we not only *have* the mind of Christ, we are *operating* with His mind.

Paul asks if we are confident in this. Can you possibly imagine what the Holy Spirit can show you when your mind is submitted to Him? The imagination is a beautiful gift from God and allows us to be "taken up" with Him at any moment. There is no limit; it is all up to Him if we can surrender our heart and mind fully to Him.

Did you know that John experienced all five senses in Revelation?

John was *in the Spirit*, which indicates supernatural revelation through a vision and a real experience. Our visions, no doubt, flow through our imagination. Did you know it is impossible to build or invent anything without imagining it first?

About 13 years ago I asked the Holy Spirit to describe John's experience to me. I was asking Him for a word. I had my own experiences, but I wanted a definition for it. When I asked Him, He said the word "spheritual" to me. That's not in the dictionary, but I understood it to be a combination of "spiritual" and "sphere." When I looked the word meanings up it was fitting.

Sphere – (1) the apparent surface of the heavens of which half forms the dome of the visible sky. (2) any of the concentric and acentric revolving spherical transparent shells in which according to ancient astronomy stars, sun, planets, and moon are set.

Spiritual – (1) relating to, consisting of, or affecting the spirit. (2) relating to sacred matters (3) related or joined in spirit.

Spheritual – (my simple definition) where the Spirit meets the atmosphere of the heavens.

Interestingly enough, I did see the word recently, related to a kid's game and someone's art work. But I will give "spheritual" its due definition and respect according to what the Holy Spirit said it was to me back in 2004.

I believe John had a spheritual experience in Revelation and I believe anyone can. Remember when I shared that I have a mental shelf where I put things that I question, don't agree with, or don't understand? If you are struggling with what I am saying you might want to put it on your mental shelf and revisit this later. John experienced all five senses through his spheritual experience.

"I was in the Spirit on the Lord's Day, and I heard behind me a loud voice like the sound of a trumpet," – Revelation 1:10

He goes on to see and witness many things all throughout Revelation, and is told to write it down. He *heard*; he *saw*; he *felt* the hand of the Lord touch him; there were bowls of incense which he *smelled*; and he *tasted* the scroll sweet to his mouth and sour on his stomach. There is so much to read of his experience. Was it any less of an experience because he wasn't transported in the physical body? Of course not; he was taken up in the vision the Lord had given him. How amazing! We have so much to be thankful for in all that John revealed to us in the book of Revelation.

We too have it all available to us, as children of God. Though John was chosen as a scribe for the Spirit of the Lord, we too are chosen. Aren't we to be witnesses of the Lord in all that we say and do? Yes, both physically and in the Spirit.

Years ago, we were having a prayer meeting at our ministry base. We were being quiet before the Lord and I had prayed that we would submit our hearts and minds to the Holy Spirit; that He would meet us in our minds. When we were done, I asked if anyone had an experience with the Lord they wanted to share. One girl described a heavenly meeting with the Lord in a beautiful place among trees. The pathway that she walked down was *exactly* the same as I had also experienced many times before. We talked about it and took turns describing the scene. How good of the Lord to confirm the beauty of heaven through two of us in the group with identical experiences. This has happened many times since, where I've witnessed the Lord giving the same experience to different people. Why does He do this? It is of course to confirm that He is real, and that the kingdom of heaven is within our grasp here on earth.

We don't have to be afraid of the mysteries of heaven. If they are lining up with God's Word then we know that we are in His boat. The Bible is our rudder and will keep steering us in the right direction, as we are careful to make room in our boat for the Holy Spirit to reveal Himself in new ways. Though He cannot be put in a box, we can certainly put ourselves in one. The Holy Spirit is incapable of being confined. If we are diligently seeking the Lord, He may show us a bit of the vastness of who He is.

When my boys were young, they attended a co-op home school where we lived. The parents traded off days to teach and I taught art and prayer to the kids. One day, I had them all sit down. We got still and quiet. I shared with them Matthew 22:37, and that Jesus wanted to love them and be loved by them through their hearts and minds. We invited the Holy Spirit to come and be with us. Then I told them we would sit still and remain quiet with our eyes closed, as we went to our favorite place with Jesus in our minds. I used Lectio Divina as my teaching tool and asked them to use all of their senses through Matthew 22:37. It was so powerful. God blessed us all beyond what I could have imagined. Some of the kids shared that they played basketball with Jesus. Some played video games with Him. Some walked along the beach with Him, or swam with

Him. It was incredible. Not every child shared, but most of them did. When they talked about how it made them feel, they were all so happy and encouraged. They had their own experience with Jesus. Though it was in the Spirit, it was very real. Praise Him!

Hopefully this gives us a fresh fire to reach out to the lost and those around us. They are helpless and hopeless, and need Jesus as their Savior. Without Jesus they are powerless to conquer sin and death. Without Him their imaginations are given over to themselves and the world. There are people plagued daily with nightmares and tormented by the enemy. Jesus wants to set them free. It is by His Spirit that we can conquer a mind that is enslaved by the enemy. Hallelujah!

12 – Faith

Therefore, I say to you, all things for which you pray and ask, believe that you have received them, and they will be granted to you. – Mark 11:24

No one begins their relationship with the Lord without faith. It was faith that made you say "yes" to Him as your Lord and Savior, faith that leads you to read His Word, and it was even with faith that you picked up this little book. Any step towards God begins with faith.

"Now faith is the assurance of things hoped for, the conviction of things not seen." – Hebrews 11:1

"And without faith it is impossible to please Him, for he who comes to God must believe that He is and that He is a rewarder of those who seek Him." – Hebrews 11:6

I believe the story of Abraham taking his son Isaac to the altar of sacrifice exemplifies the most tested faith ever. Abraham's is an amazing testimony of hearing God tell him to do something, and knowing that He would provide a solution, regardless of what Abraham had to prove through obedience. And with his child, too! I can't imagine. This is why God was pleased with Abraham. His obedience went beyond his love for his own son, and of course serves as such a beautiful illustration of what the Father did for us through Jesus.

Our expression of faith is for ourselves and for others to see, not for God's benefit. God knows the hearts of men. He does not require that we prove anything to Him for His benefit. He is all-knowing. When we read in Scripture that He tested people, or asked them a question, it was for their benefit; He already knew their actions and answers. Still, walking out our obedience in faith and then seeing the outcome is part of our training and it pleases Him. Tests are always for our benefit and are meant to encourage us, spur us on, and build our faith. Faith is for our assurance, our hope, our convictions, and our belief (Hebrews 11:1-6.)

Our failure to walk in obedient faith will sometimes mean we have to go around the same mountain again. The Lord knows what we need and never looks at failure the way we do.

"And He said to them, 'Because of the littleness of your faith; for truly I say to you, if you have faith the size of a mustard seed, you will say to this mountain, "Move from here to there," and it will move; and nothing will be impossible to you.'"
– Matthew 17:20

Why is it so hard for us to stir up such little faith, the size of a mustard seed? It seems that such little faith would be simple, yet there is a real reason why so many of us struggle with it, or can't obtain it.

"So faith comes by hearing, and hearing by the Word of Christ." – Romans 10:17

The simple truth is God's people are not feeding on and hearing the Word enough, through their own personal study or in gatherings with other believers. If we are not reading the Word or hearing the Word, how can our faith increase? Without faith, we are sitting ducks for any of life's many trials to take hold of us and remove all hope. Without faith we are hopeless, unable to receive God's love and believe He is who He says He is, and powerless to overcome the world. I can't imagine anything more devastating other than Hell itself.

"Who is it that overcomes the world, but the one that believes that Jesus is the Son of God?" – 1 John 5:5

Living by faith is allowing Jesus to move through us and work through us, His life for ours, His power for our submission. Faith allows the deep love of God to be made manifest in us and through us. When we receive Jesus as Lord and Savior and give Him permission to become LORD over our lives, we no longer live as our old selves. Jesus becomes Lord as well as Savior. His *salvation*, of course, was only the beginning purpose of His coming, but His *lordship* means He is *Ruler* and *King* in our lives. We allow Him to take our lives over, His life for ours.

"I have been crucified with Christ; and it is no longer I who live, but Christ lives in me; and the life which I now live in the flesh I live by faith in the Son of God, who loved me and gave Himself up for me." – Galatians 2:20

This verse is a declaration that every Christian should say regularly. It is a reminder that by faith we walk with the indwelling Spirit of God daily. Hallelujah!

What else can destroy faith?

As a believer in Jesus there are two types of death for us. We are either dying to our flesh so that He can live through us, *or* we are truly dying and deteriorating from sinful living and slipping away from our salvation.

This book would be meaningless if I didn't discuss the things that can demolish our ability to walk by faith and grow in our relationship with the Lord.

So many amazing Christians are entertaining sin in their daily walk and habits. We are *all* being cleaned up by the love and goodness of Jesus. If we are forever changing into the likeness of Jesus, then what we got away with a year ago, a month ago, will not be allowed now.

Some are watching horror movies, listening to evil music, playing demonic video games, watching sexual perversion shows, eating junk food, smoking, and drinking (I'm not talking about the occasional drink). Some are allowing other religions to mix within their heart and mind, and letting offenses and anger take hold, making them powerless.

How effective will our growth in our relationship with Jesus be if we allow these behaviors to go on? We must ask ourselves, "As the world falls more apart every day, am I ready for what is to come?" We are not ready if we are practicing habits like those listed above. These kinds of activities will demolish our faith. Why? Because with each act of sin we push the righteousness of Jesus further and further away. As this happens, it is harder and harder to become like Him. If we are living sinful lives we are dying.

"And you were dead in your trespasses and sins, in which you formerly walked according to the course of this world, according to the prince of the power of the air, of the spirit that is now working in the sons of disobedience. Among them we too all formerly lived in the lusts of our flesh, indulging the desires of the flesh and of the mind, and were by nature children of wrath, even as the rest. But God, being rich in mercy, because of His great love with which He loved us, even when we were dead in our transgressions, made us alive together with Christ (by grace you have been saved), and raised us up with Him, and seated us with Him in the heavenly places in Christ Jesus, so that in the ages to come He might show the surpassing riches of His grace in kindness toward us in Christ Jesus. For by grace you have been saved through faith; and that not of yourselves, it is the gift of God; not as a result of works, so that no one may boast. For we are His workmanship, created in Christ Jesus for good works, which God prepared beforehand so that we would walk in them." – Ephesians 2:1-10

This is absolutely amazing. It says that as we are new in Christ we are *in* Jesus and "seated with Him in the heavenly places!" He will show us His riches of grace and kindness, and even more because of His grace and mercy over us. We are truly set for eternity as we continue to grow in Him.

It's also clear that if we are living a life of sin we are "sons of disobedience" indulging in the sins of the flesh and waiting on wrath. This is by our doing, not His. God has given us His all, His beautiful Son as our life boat so that every one of us may be saved.

I know without a shadow of a doubt that anyone in hell will be there because they want to be, because they chose to be. God is so merciful, so loving, so caring, He became our answer in every way, demolishing *every* scheme of the enemy to destroy us. Yet, there are so many that blame God for their circumstances which are actually the consequences of their own actions. I know many people trapped in this mindset. To blame God is the ultimate escape from their own responsibilities or the cruel nature of the world. It is a sad and bitter existence when we blame God out of our own pride; pride that keeps us from admitting our mistakes; owning our own bad choices, or recognizing a fallen world with an agenda to steer us away from God who is the only One who can save us.

So why does God allow starving children? Abused children? Evil upon evil? He allows it as He put the responsibility in the hands of His children, Christians! As He died on the Cross He said "It is finished." All was finished and completed, and it was now for us to walk out what He told us to do with the Great Commission. He told us to "heal the sick, raise the dead, and cast out demons." He has given us all we need to go and do it. Do we even realize the world is the way it is because the Body of Christ has not unified to do its job? Sadly, we don't hear much preaching on these subjects.

So why are Christians so far from doing what we've been told to do by Jesus? Mostly because so many are destroying their faith with their daily lives as we've already discussed. It makes it impossible to walk in the power of the Holy Spirit. Jesus even said that *He* couldn't heal in His hometown because of their lack of faith (Mark 6:5).

All that said, I believe we are entering into the greatest harvest time of miracles the Church has ever seen. I believe the Holy Spirit is wooing people to want more of Him. Do you sense He is wooing you? I believe if we answer the promptings of the

Holy Spirit in our lives, we will see His goodness like never before.

"'And it shall be in the last days,' God says,
'That I will pour out My Spirit on all mankind;
And your sons and your daughters will prophesy,
And your young men will see visions,
And your old men will have dreams;

And even on My male and female servants
I will pour out My Spirit in those days,
And they shall prophesy.

And I will display wonders in the sky above
And signs on the earth below,
Blood, and fire, and vapor of smoke.

The sun will be turned into darkness
And the moon into blood,
Before the great and glorious day of the Lord comes.

And it shall be that everyone who calls on the name of the Lord will be saved.'" – Acts 2:17-21

You might ask yourself serious questions…

> Do I want to go deeper in my relationship with the Lord or am I content where I am?

Do I want to heal the sick, cast out demons and raise people up from the dead?

These are hard questions. We need to be totally honest with ourselves because Jesus already knows the answers. Any answer other than wanting to go deeper with the Lord and do His will means something is off in our life. Let us all make the decision to deal with what has a grip on our heart and mind. Dying to our fleshly desires will escalate our faith! It will catapult it into another level of understanding and power.

I once had an experience when I was very young, too young, 8th grade. I was not a wild kid, but I had a wild moment. I had partied too hard with my friends and was terribly sick from drinking. I threw up all over my friend's kitchen; it was terrible. The next day I had a family function and while my parents were driving to it, I lay miserable in the back seat of the car. As I was trying to act normal, I had a vision. I saw what looked like a "Y." I did not hear an audible voice of the Lord but He spoke as He planted within my spirit an automatic *knowing* and fear. The "Y" represented two paths of my life, a crossroads. This was just something I knew and understood in the moment. The "Y" was a fork in the road of my life, one direction was Life and one was Death. I knew that I would literally die if I went down the "party path." I'm not saying that I was an angel afterward, but that moment certainly changed my life. It was always in the back of my mind in all that I did.

Are you at a crossroads with the above questions?

If you have no desire to go deeper in your relationship with the Lord, or to do His will, then pray and ask Jesus to give you His desires.

I am forever grateful for the Fear of the Lord that dropped in my heart that day as it prompted an understanding of faith in my life. That experience planted faith real enough to not dismiss it. The experience made an imprint on my soul.

I believe every person gets a similar moment or sign in their life but most do not choose to recognize it as a warning sign. It is easy to just call it "life" and go on. These types of wake-up calls in our lives, if heeded, pave the way and allow decisions of faith to take place. Faith to know what we see and feel in our moment of truth is real and very defining for our lives.

"Blessed are they who did not see, and yet believe" – John 20:29

Faith is a gift that the Holy Spirit uses to guide us in the direction He wants us to go. Faith is directly linked to our obedience to Him. It pleases Him, and in return He rewards us! He's a good, good Father.

"And without faith it is impossible to please Him, for he who comes to God must believe that He is and that He is a rewarder of those who seek Him." – Hebrews 11:6

Faith lives when our flesh dies. God has a plan and a purpose for our lives and faith will keep us on His path to finish the race!

Years ago, when my husband was let go from his job and came home to tell me, he shared, "I got let go today from my job." I gasped with fear. Then he said, "Honey, they couldn't help but hire me, and they couldn't help but let me go, because I belong to Jesus." It totally extinguished the fear that the enemy tried to bring; instead, it brought faith. Little did I know that was the beginning of Jesus calling us to full-time missions.

After that, Mike applied for many jobs and started two side businesses -- a computer consulting business and a photography business. For nine months we prayed and prayed, but each time he applied for a job, he was over-qualified. People were giving us gas cards and grocery cards; it was a humbling time. We had no idea the Lord was teaching us to receive as training for the mission field.

Finally, I became angry with the Lord. I had never been angry at God before. I went into my room, lay on the bed and threw a temper tantrum before God, telling Him of my anger. We had done all we knew to do. We were faithful but still no job had been found. I cried out, "What do you want, Lord?" At that moment in His loving quiet voice He said, "I want it all, Caron." I responded loudly, "Well, You can have it all!!!" It's funny now, but it certainly wasn't at the time. After I said that, I knew in my Spirit that He was calling us to full-time missions. It was just dropped down into my Spirit and I understood He was speaking to me.

I lay there crying, soaking in what I had heard. Mike had been in his office in the other room and walked in while I was crying. I said to him, "Michael, I believe the Lord is calling us to be missionaries." He said, "I know, He just told me the same thing." It was a profound moment for both of us. We had never discussed missions before. We had some acquaintances that were missionaries, but it was never something that we had thought about for ourselves or our family. It began a journey of dying to ourselves and walking by faith that we could never have imagined or wanted. How good of the Lord to speak to us both simultaneously. Our faith came by us hearing.

It was a year of planning after that, with many stories of faith and God's amazing provision. He showed us His power and led us through the pain of leaving family, friends, and our comforts. It was a precious, bittersweet time that I'd do all over again. Thanks be to Jesus.

13 – Abiding in Jesus

Anyone who goes too far and does not remain in the teaching of Christ, does not have God; the one who abides in the teaching, he has both the Father and the Son. – 2 John 1:9

Abiding – continuing for a long time: Enduring.

Endure – to continue in the same state; to remain firm under suffering without yielding.

Jesus has told us to abide in Him. From the definitions of these words, He wants us to continue with Him for a long time and *endure* with Him in whatever life throws at us. The picture painted by these definitions may not at first seem to be a pretty one, but I believe it is beautiful.

To abide in Jesus is to have an ongoing prayer life, building an enduring relationship, rather than one that is periodic or intermittent. As with any relationship, there will definitely be hardship and suffering, but His love and promises keep us sustained. Jesus was never shy about telling us we would suffer for His sake, since He also suffered. His suffering is completed; our hardships come with picking up our daily cross and walking with Him.

"I am the true vine, and My Father is the vinedresser. [2] Every branch in Me that does not bear fruit, He takes away; and every branch that bears fruit, He prunes it so that it may bear more fruit. [3] You are already clean because of the word which I have spoken to you. [4] Abide in Me, and I in you. As the branch cannot bear fruit of itself unless it abides in the vine, so neither can you unless you abide in Me. [5] I am the vine, you are the branches; he who abides in Me and I in him, he bears much fruit, for apart from Me you can do nothing. [6] If anyone does not abide in Me, he is thrown away as a branch and dries up; and they gather them, and cast them into the fire and they are burned. [7] If you abide in Me, and My words abide in you, ask whatever you wish, and it will be done for you. [8] My Father is glorified by this, that you bear much fruit, and so prove to be My disciples. [9] Just as the Father has loved Me, I have also loved you; abide in My love. [10] If you keep My commandments, you will abide in My love; just as I have kept My Father's commandments and abide in His love. [11] These things I have spoken to you so that My joy may be in you, and that your joy may be made full." – John 15:1-11

As Jesus is the true vine, anything other than Him that grabs our hearts and minds first, is false. This shows us that there may be many things to examine in our lives that do not prove to follow after the righteousness of Jesus. There will be many false vines, things we attach ourselves to that produce a different kind of fruit. If we are constantly listening to bad music that promotes selfishness or sexual promiscuity then it will take root in our heart and mind and begin to produce bad fruit that leads to death.

Jesus says that "My Father is the vinedresser." The role of a vinedresser is to *daily* prune and cultivate the vines. This is important for the production of good fruit and wine.

As awkward as some might feel when reading it, the entire seventh chapter of Song of Solomon is a beautiful description of how the Lord views the Church, His bride. There are several references in this chapter to grapes, the vine, and wine being like the bride of Christ. There is nothing strange about it; its description is perfect and righteous. The Father is preparing us to be a beautiful bride for His Son, the One who is worthy.

Looking at John 15, we see the warning that comes from not abiding in Jesus. He says that any branch not bearing fruit will be thrown away. This might sound harsh but this is the Father pruning and preparing us for His Son. He knows our hearts, our desires and intentions. He throws us away if we've rejected His Son and *chosen* to not abide. Also, we have to understand how righteous Jesus is; He is sinless and can't be adjoined to sin. This is why when he looks at us, His born-again children, He ultimately sees Himself over us; it's His righteousness in Himself *and* *in* *us* that is His finished product (2 Corinthians 5:21).

He prepared the way for us on the cross that we may choose to walk blameless with Him every day; it is our choice. It IS possible to not sin. And when we do sin, a lifestyle of repentance allows us to walk daily in His grace. Remember, if we repent, our sin is thrown as far as the East is to the West and will be remembered no more (Psalms 103:12).

It is ultimately our choice: a lifestyle of obedience, repentance and grace, or a life that rejects Christ and has no lasting fruit. For those who choose the latter, the Father throws away. Let's look at what it says next, in verse 6. "…they gather them up and cast them into the fire to be burned."

Who is "they"?

Anyone who has not attached himself to the Vine (that is, Jesus) has most certainly attached himself to the devil and the "sons" of disobedience. They will be the ones at liberty to gather up the "discarded branches." Scary but true!

If we are abiding in Jesus we are attached to His life, His desires and His plans. We will put our fleshly desires aside to walk out the life of Jesus.

We see in verse 7 that abiding in Him allows His words to be living and active within us. He is the Word incarnate, and we can ask whatever we will, according to His Word, and it will be done for us. This is so powerful. It is my own experience that we don't have to act on much faith, just a mustard seed's worth will shift and move mountains. Truly.

I believe one of the biggest assaults on our understanding of abiding in Jesus is the high rate of divorce among Christians. We have truly lost our way in our marriages because we "deserve" to be happy. We have lost the understanding of what it means to be long suffering, enduring one another at all costs. Some may not like reading this. I'm for sure not talking about the abusive marriage, or even infidelity, but the daily struggle to just stay married. We are always looking for the fairy tale, looking for love in the wrong places. Only Jesus is our true fairy tale, or, as I prefer to call Him, our dream come true.

The unrealistic demands we have put on our marriages have trickled into our relationships with Jesus. We are impatient and try to make demands on Him. We are an entitled people, especially in America. We want what we want and we want it now. If we don't get what we want or our prayers are not answered the way we think they should be, we blame Him for it. Our Lord is not one to be told what to do and He certainly doesn't cater to our fits and stubbornness. He loves us so much that He will allow the pain to come; He will allow the refining fire to burn as long as it takes to bring us to the end of ourselves, in order that He can be Lord of our lives. Still, He has given us free will and sits back knowing that usually we only run to Him when we are in need or great pain. It hurts Him deeply to see His children walk through a divorce. It's a direct attack on His divine plan of love, and we are all His Bride. Our marriages are to be a reflection of our marriage to Him. He knows all too well the understanding of abiding, endurance, and long suffering. He will never divorce us. He is in it for good, and has already paid the ultimate price for a successful marriage with us.

14 – Our New Identity

I have been crucified with Christ; and it is no longer I who live, but Christ lives in me; and the life which I now live in the flesh I live by faith in the Son of God, who loved me and gave Himself up for me. – *Galatians 2:20*

As we invite Jesus to be our Lord and Savior, we enter into an agreement with Him, His life and His identity for ours. We've said this, but at some point it will click within us that as we belong to Him, it is *His* life to be walked out. Jesus has given us His *whole* identity by His Spirit. This is such a huge thing for us to grasp. In the flesh we have limited understanding of what this actually means, but by the Spirit the meaning is infinite and immeasurable.

The temptation is for us as Christians to believe that we are just people who have to deal with life as it is dealt to us: sickness, disease, divorce, at times helplessness. This is what those living in the world witness daily. The enemy would want us to believe this to keep us powerless and accepting of all circumstances.

Walking in our new identity means we have the same power as Jesus did. Do you believe that? He said that we would do even greater things.

"Truly, truly, I say to you, he who believes in Me, the works that I do, he will do also; and greater works than these, he will do; because I go to the Father. Whatever you ask in My name, that will I do, so that the Father may be glorified in the Son. If you ask Me anything in My name, I will do it." – John 14:12-14

Our new identity comes with a calling for every one of us. Jesus said,

"Go therefore and make disciples of all the nations, baptizing them in the name of the Father and the Son and the Holy Spirit, teaching them to observe all that I commanded you; and lo, I am with you always, even to the end of the age." – Matthew 28:19

As Jesus says this to His disciples, He says it to us too; *we* are His disciples. Does this mean that as we become Christians, we are to leave our country and go to another? Not necessarily. It could mean that we just walk across the street, teach Sunday School class, or host a Bible study in our home. This is where prayer and listening to the Lord is needed so that we do what He tells us to. The point is, we are sharing Jesus with others, no matter where we are. This is a command from Jesus to ALL of His children. We are all missionaries, but with that said, we are forever being discipled by the Holy Spirit. We are His students first, sitting at His feet and learning daily how to become like Him. We are His light.

The mission organization with which we work, YWAM (Youth With A Mission), practices this principle: first do, then teach. As we learn to sit in the presence of the Lord and pray, study His word, and be filled up with His power, we then show others how to do the same. To do this means we practice. If we sense we are lacking in an area and know we need more experience, we can search out those who are operating in the area in which we are weak. This is what we did as a family. We went to YWAM for more teaching and training.

I remember when the Lord called us to leave for missions. I was faced with such inadequacies. I didn't think I was "qualified" to go anywhere for Jesus. He then showed me my pride in those thoughts. To think on myself and my feelings isn't putting Jesus at the center of His calling in my life.

I soon realized that a surrendered vessel to Jesus is a useful vessel, no matter who it is. It is He who qualifies us to do anything at all by His Spirit and for the Kingdom. By this time, I had learned a lifestyle of sitting in His presence and was ready to walk it out in power. Jesus said to "heal the sick, cast out demons, and raise the dead." I knew this was the direction I was going. I wanted *all* of Jesus, no matter how intimidated I might have been!

The other part of Matthew 28:19 is "teaching them to observe all that I commanded you." We can try to just do the first part but if we are not also doing the "teaching them" part, we are not being fully obedient. Not only are we to share the love of Jesus and lead others to Him, but we are also to make sure they become His disciples.

It is a beautiful and wonderful thing to see mega gatherings for the Kingdom, sharing the Gospel and seeing so many come into the Family of God, but if we are not willing to exercise the other part of the commandment of discipleship and teaching them, we might be doing more harm than good. To bring someone into the Kingdom and then leave them reminds me of a one-night stand, "love'em and leave'em." We have taken advantage of the Holy Spirit's prompting to lead a person to salvation through Him, then left them vulnerable to the attacks of the devil. This is a horrible witness of the nurturing heart of the Lord and it happens often.

Jesus cares for us. He promises to never leave us nor forsake us, and He expects us to be a reflection of Him as we reach out to others. If a new believer doesn't know that Jesus promises to never leave them then they will feel more alone than before. We have to be willing to baptize them, and to teach them what we know of the Lord, just as Matthew 28 tells us to do.

Having an identity in Jesus is about being His disciple and hearing His voice, with a calling on our life -- a calling to make more disciples and teach them to also walk in His identity.

Loving others and teaching them about Jesus is not easy but is full of blessings. If you are willing to spend time with Him daily, walk by faith and be obedient to what He tells you to do then there is nothing that can't be done through you by His Spirit.

It takes time to believe that we are who God says we are. Practicing walking it out allows our faith to be exercised. Faith and identity in Jesus go hand in hand. It's a pretty miraculous thought to know that we are created in the image of God. That alone is huge! Even though all of this revelation takes time to soak into our hearts and minds, we are learning on the job. We are living and active beings, just as the Word is living and active. (Hebrews 4:12) Few things in our walk with Jesus come instantaneously, but how nice when it does happen.

In the Stillness

15 – Psalms 46:10

Be still and know that I am God; I will be exalted among the nations, I will be exalted in the earth. – Psalms 46:10

As you can see from having two chapters around Psalm 46:10, it is my favorite verse. It is a direct reflection of what is produced from the stillness, from taking time to be in His presence daily. This verse comes with a promise and it all has to do with Jesus and His evangelizing heart for all people. If we take time to be still in His presence, then He is exalted among the nations and the whole earth. It sounds so simple, doesn't it? I believe that it is supposed to be. He is saying that out of the stillness comes the finished goal and that nothing else will do. All we have to do is spend time with Him. It goes so well with "But seek first His kingdom and His righteousness, and all these things will be added to you."

It is only from the stillness that we can obtain His righteousness. If we are seeking Him whole-heartedly, the outcome is that everything else in life falls into place. We will *want* to make Him known, we will *want* to share the Gospel, and we *will* walk by faith. In the stillness our identity becomes

His and He will move our hearts as His did. We will walk by faith in obedience to Him.

As I've shared from my own experiences, one of the best ways to walk out our faith is to get involved in a prayer group. If your church doesn't have a prayer group, then start one, or find one within your community. There is truly nothing more empowering than praying with a body of believers for something that is on God's heart to be established. When we begin to see answers to prayers come forth, it not only encourages our faith, but we are witnessing a real move of God happening as we agree together. It is the best kind of unity. Through prayer, we have power where otherwise we may be powerless. Some examples might be our family, our church, state, government, nation, and many more areas. Praying with others spurs us on to let go of worry or anxiety. To tackle an issue together and leave it at the feet of Jesus is trusting Him and saying that we are not capable. Corporate humility is corporate power.

Over the years I've seen countless prayers answered where there were two or more of us pouring our hearts out, asking, declaring and standing on God's Word in prayer. A prayer life is nothing short of exciting!

"Be anxious for nothing, but in everything by prayer and supplication with thanksgiving let your requests be made known to God." – Philippians 4:6

Notice that again in this verse there is thanksgiving. As we discussed earlier, a heart of thanksgiving gives all glory to God and does not accredit anything to man's doing. A thankful heart trusts the Lord for all that we are going through, good or bad, knowing that He's orchestrating our life. It's also a slap in the face to the enemy who would make us worry and become bitter with a heart of entitlement. As we pray together, we combat those fleshly desires as well. With thankful hearts we can approach the Father, making our requests known in confidence (1 John 5:14-15.)

"Again I say to you, that if two of you agree on earth about anything that they may ask, it shall be done for them by My Father who is in heaven." – Matthew 18:19

For every believer there will be a time of stretching as the Lord calls us to walk out our identity and calling in Him by going somewhere, teaching, or in some way sharing the Gospel and love of Jesus. If you consider yourself to be a "seasoned" Christian and have yet to do anything to stretch your faith for the Kingdom by sharing the Gospel, then you might be behind. Align yourself with your church, and if you don't have a church, find one! It is so important to be able to serve on some level with your church, have a sense of belonging by sowing into that body of believers. To go somewhere and serve (on a missions trip, for example), to have experiences sharing Jesus with others, is to become *family* and bring others into the Family. You will be amazed at how much you learn and enjoy it. Being out of our comfort zones for Christ is part of true Christianity. The Lord will no doubt ask us to do things that we cannot possibly do on our own. This enables us to humble ourselves, and allows Him to receive all the glory. He will never ask or prompt us to do anything that He has not equipped us for. Not by might nor power but by His Spirit. It is never too late to be called by Jesus, and we are never too old to serve. He makes us capable.

One of my first experiences of walking in the power of the Lord took place in another country and was way out of my comfort zone. We were staying at an orphanage. These children were horribly abused and every one of them had been sexually assaulted, sold, or used. Their ages ranged from 1–18 years old.

When we arrived at the orphanage, we were told about a little 5-year-old boy that lived there and who was very angry. He lashed out at people, growled at them and would bite them. Let's say his name was Ronnie. Not long after we arrived, I had my first encounter with little Ronnie. He jumped out from behind a bush and growled and hissed at me. Some people would try and analyze this child incessantly, saying his behavior was psychosomatic from all the trauma in his life, but as soon as I saw him the Holy Spirit told me he was possessed by multiple demons. Now, remember that little mental shelf we talked about, you might put this on it until we chat further.

So little Ronnie was full of demons and acting out towards me, and I am sure towards others, for some time. It was truly sad to see. I was willing to do something about it if the Lord would put me in the right situation with this little boy. Since we were guests on the orphanage property, we had to respect their leadership's requests of us and were told that no one was allowed to be alone with any orphan. I believe this was a good rule, considering the trauma the children had endured.

After we had been there a couple weeks, one of the workers was having a baby shower and I was invited. I sat in the room enjoying the party when little Ronnie came through the door. He wasn't acting out but just looking around the room. Everyone there was so used to his behavior they didn't pay him any attention. I didn't even notice that anyone else saw him walk in the room. Then Ronnie stared straight into my eyes and came walking towards me. Holy Spirit said to me, "Pick him up and hold him tight against you and tell the demons to leave." Ronnie was a little thing, weighing probably forty pounds, so I knew I could do this but was I nervous? YES!

Still, the Holy Spirit told me to do it so I did. I quickly picked him up on my lap. As I was sitting in the corner, I stretched him across the front of me and held him as tight as I could. No one was even paying me any attention as they were fixed on the newborn baby at the shower. Ronnie began to pull and squirm; I just held him tighter. I leaned over and said quietly in his ear, "You demons get out of this boy right now in the name of Jesus." Ronnie squirmed and huffed with his breath and I KNEW they had left him! I then began speaking love over him and telling him Jesus loved him. I asked the Holy Spirit to come and dwell in those places within Ronnie that had once held demons. I just kept praying over him, loving him and I kissed his cheek while still holding him tight.

I knew Ronnie didn't speak English but it didn't matter. I trusted the Holy Spirit to interpret for me and knew that He'd take care of that part. Ronnie just stared at me with the most precious look and smile through his little rotten teeth. His eyes were lit up; he looked like a different child. I finally let him get up; he was smiling as he ran out the door. I never said a word to anyone about it as the Lord told me not to, except to my husband.

Over the next few days there were several local workers talking about Ronnie and how different he was. Ronnie would just smile when he came near me, and he'd wait for me to hug him tight. I never again saw him growl or misbehave while I was there, for two whole months! That little boy was set free in a moment's notice. The demonic stronghold that had been over him, and I'm sure had come in through the sexual assaults and abuse, had been broken. When I look back on it, it was simple. There was no screaming or yelling; the enemy recognized Jesus in me and had to leave. Thanks be to God! This was part of my new identity. It was trusting Jesus to manifest through me as I was obedient to Him.

This story, and countless others, would not be possible if I didn't have a prayer life and recognize the voice of the Lord. It is ALL for Him and all glory and praise be to Him. This too is for anyone and everyone who wants to do the will of their Lord and Savior Jesus.

16 – Spiritual Warfare & Fear

But, the Lord is faithful, and He will strengthen and protect you from the evil one. – 2 Thessalonians 3:3

When walking in the identity of Jesus and by His Spirit, we can expect the devil's resistance. Though we can't blame the enemy for everything, we can certainly blame him for a lot. He has made it his job to resist the Kingdom of God and its growth. There is little time left for him and he knows it. The devil is a show boat; his job is to intimidate us through fear. He can totally accomplish this if we Christians are rocked in our identity in Jesus. As we've discussed already, if we don't know who we are in Christ, the devil can remind us of who we aren't and we won't have the confidence to stand against him. Fear debilitates us and that is the goal of the enemy.

Through prayer and waiting in the stillness with Jesus, we allow the voice of the Lord to become the loudest, and it drowns out the voices of the enemy. We have to learn to ignore the enemy and his tactics, capture the thoughts of fear, and remind him of who we are and who he isn't! Remember, he is a created being just like we are and ALL the power that he uses belongs to God; it will soon be revoked!

Did you know that the words "Fear not" are in the Bible 365 times, one for each day of the year? The Word tells us we are to be alert against the enemy's attacks but never fearful.

"Be of sober spirit, be on the alert. Your adversary, the devil, prowls around like a roaring lion, seeking someone to devour." – 1 Peter 5:8

I find it interesting that so many Christians struggle with believing in spiritual warfare when it's constantly around us. I think we just have to turn on the TV and see the horror in entertainment to get a glimpse of how the devil is working 24/7 to keep people shackled in sin and darkness. Like I said earlier, we can't blame the devil for everything, especially when we are making the bad decisions to watch the horror on TV, drink until we are drunk, and listen to the negative music, watch the porn, cuss, and more. Those are our decisions; still, the devil makes sure that we live in an environment that makes us vulnerable. Our goal is to change our environment and strengthen the life and voice of God within us.

The devil can't stand an environment that radiates God's love, light, and truth.

"But they who wait for the Lord shall renew their strength; they shall mount up with wings like eagle; they shall run and not be weary; they shall walk and not faint." – Isaiah 40:31

As we wait upon the Lord, we change our environment because we give the Holy Spirit opportunity to bring more light within us and His light chases the darkness away (John 1:5). Jesus is the true light that enlightens every man.

"There was the true light which, coming into the world, enlightens every man." – John 1:9

Jesus was the light of the world and passed that torch to us, His children; now we are His light in the world (John 9:5).

If we want to change our environment, we have to share His light. Jesus promised that as He is the light, whoever follows Him will not walk in darkness, but will have the light of life.

"I have come into the world as a light, so that no one who believes in me should stay in darkness." – John 12:46

It is impossible for the devil to dwell where the light is. This may be hard for some of us to understand, especially as we see so many being martyred for the sake of the Gospel. Even in martyrdom, the enemy is limited. The devil may take our earthly life but he knows he can't touch our salvation. Our life and the light of Jesus can never be snuffed out.

Where the light of Jesus is, no devil can rule in fear unless we give him permission. Where light is, there is the love of Jesus and His perfect love casts out fear (1 John 4:18). There is no condemnation towards anyone in this statement as we watch our brothers and sisters being martyred daily around the world.

I can't imagine the fear the enemy brings in those moments. We the Church must continue to pray for them, for strength to endure until the end.

As Christians, it's our job to rise up with the authority of Jesus and command darkness to leave. If we will do this, it has to obey. Day by day, we can intentionally invite the Light, or, with our words and actions, invite the darkness. As love and light live within us, so we have the power to change our environment.

Once when we were in Liberia, Africa, my husband and I were ministering to a group of people. Most of them professed to be Christians, but some were from a village where there was a witch doctor. As we were praying over people, some began to cry out to the Lord and weep. One woman came to us asking for prayer. She said the witch doctor had put a spell on her and that her head was splitting in two. She suffered from horrible headaches and wanted freedom. She was terrified that her head would literally split in two because this is what the witch doctor had told her would happen. She professed to be a Christian, and we explained to her that she is not subject to the things or demons of this world, but that she had all she needed to overcome the darkness and witchcraft from the witch doctor. This "spell" from the witch doctor was a form of spiritual warfare that had snared her through fear. We prayed for her and rebuked the evil oppression from the witch doctor and she immediately began to feel better. Still, this was an attack on her identity, and she will have to stay in the Word and before the Lord in order to keep her true identity and healing. It is not by might or power but by His Spirit (Zechariah 4:6). The devil will always try and rob us of our healings and our freedoms.

"You are from God, little children, and have overcome them; because greater is He who is in you than he who is in the world." – 1 John 4:4

The demonic forces that promote fear around us are real, but with the spiritual authority of Jesus we have the power to cast them out (Luke 10:19). There is no other way to combat spiritual warfare and fear than to sit in the stillness with Jesus.

So how do we begin to change our atmosphere? There is nothing better than to cleanse our home and environment with worship music. Filling our home and car with a steady stream of worship will not only change the atmosphere but it will begin cleansing our heart and mind. I keep my music on daily, sometimes all day. For years I have done this and it has ministered to me and my family in beautiful ways.

"For our struggle is not against flesh and blood, but against the rulers, against the powers, against the world forces of wickedness in the heavenly places." – Ephesians 6:12

If only we could believe this verse to a depth that allows us to see the enemy, rather than the person the enemy is using. It would usher in compassion and understanding, and save all sorts of judgments. Yes, some people have given themselves over to the enemy on purpose and have no desire for true deliverance as they are not in their right minds, but many are lost and searching for Jesus.

When Jesus was among those who were possessed, He didn't ask them if they wanted or liked their demons. He just told the demons to leave. Are we not to do the same? The saying, "Hate the sin but love the sinner" is wonderful instruction but we can't do it without more love of Jesus in our hearts. Knowing who we are in Jesus doesn't depend on the freedom of others, it depends on our ability to set captives free.

17 – Prophets & Giving Prophecy Words

For no prophecy was ever produced by the will of man, but men spoke from God as they were carried along by the Holy Spirit. – 2 Peter 1:21

Well, most in the church do NOT like talking about this subject. From my experience, either people in the church have abused the prophetic office by giving false words, or they don't believe in it, or they are not walking by faith enough to step out on that big broad limb of prophecy.

This might be very foreign to some reading this, but it needs to be a normalcy within the Church. We are told to prophesy.

A prophet in the Old Testament was someone who heard directly from God, as the Holy Spirit was not released yet in man on the earth (see Acts 2). The Old Testament prophet would say, "Thus says the Lord...," and it was the authoritative word of God. They were held to strict standards of judgment. The punishment for speaking falsely on behalf of God was death.

A New Testament prophet example looks like Jesus, period. Jesus holds the highest office of a prophet and he is our best example. Though some are *called* to be prophets, we are told in Ephesians 2:20 and 4:11 that we are ALL to prophesy. Why?

The main function of prophesying is to encourage, comfort, strengthen, and edify the church. I think we can all agree that we need that.

"But the one who prophesies speaks to people for edification, exhortation, and consolation." – 1 Corinthians 14:3

Today the most important role of the prophetic office is to encourage intimacy with the Lord and prayer. Being able to be still in His presence and hear his voice enables anyone to operate in prophecy. *Anyone!*

As we are still and listening to the Holy Spirit, He might give us a word of knowledge for someone. He may tell us something personal about that person that only He can reveal to us. Sometimes we are to share it with this person, and sometimes we are not. If we do share it, it is *always* to encourage them and never to bring attention to ourselves. All credit and glory must go to Jesus.

Sometimes the Holy Spirit will give us an overall prophetic word to share with a person, or a group. Again, prophecy is to encourage others or promote a shift towards more intimacy with Jesus.

Sometimes it's a word of warning. If this is for an individual, it is to be given in private; the Lord does not shame people. If it's a warning for the Body of Christ, it can be given in a group setting.

One thing is clear: prophecy comes out of an intimate prayer life with Jesus and hearing Him speak to us. As we submit our mind and heart to the Lord, He can show us pictures about someone or something personal in our mind. When He does this it's so we can pray and encourage them. A prophecy can be pictures of the world, environment, and more. I have had countless words like this to speak over people and to others, pictures given or flashed into my mind by the Holy Spirit. How good of Him to care so much for someone else to do this so that I may speak to them and they be encouraged.

Maybe you are praying over someone and you know by the Spirit of the Lord that something happened to them as a child and God wants to free them. Or, maybe an earthquake is coming to a specific region, or another catastrophic event. As the Holy Spirit shows us these things it is always for us to pray and we only share it with others if He tells us to. The Holy Spirit is faithful and there is no reason for Him to show us things unless He expects results through us. He loves to partner with us. He is a good God.

We may ask, if the Lord is going to warn us, why doesn't He just stop certain events? The Lord's word stands firm. He tells us that if we, His children, are not crying out to Him then the rocks will (Luke 19:40.)

The earth "groans" as creation awaits the coming of the Lord. (Romans 8:19-23)

God gave us warnings in His Word of the last days and what they would be like. It was His mercy and grace to do this. He came that all shall be saved and that none should parish.

When I have taught on hearing the voice of God, and giving prophetic words, I share that probably 90% of the things the Lord shows us are for intercession only. We don't always share with someone what the Holy Spirit shows us; we just pray. The Lord expects us to pray, pray, pray about what He tells us, then we ask Him if He wants us to share it or not. Usually, we don't.

I'd like to add something here as a fair warning. One of the biggest downfalls of the prophetic office is pride. Those who are sensitive to hear the voice of the Lord and operate in a real prophetic gifting often struggle with wanting to share everything they hear, many times stroking their egos. God will always humble them. I have dealt with this myself many times, resulting in the Lord telling me to be quiet and die to my flesh so as not to steal the glory that belongs to Him.

I once had a season in a prayer group where the Lord spoke so clearly to me, giving me incredible insight about those we were praying over that had specifically come for prayer. I had clear words, clear pictures and the Lord would tell me to be quiet, and that He would reveal it through someone else. Sometimes I'd sit through most of a session until another person would finally say what I knew in the very beginning. At the time, this was a painful process but I knew what the Lord was doing in me and for that I was so grateful. My Father knew what I needed and loved me enough to correct me in my quietness. If He had not done this I would have grown in my pride and been reckless.

On the flip side, those who don't appreciate the prophetic office will often try and stifle those giving prophetic words because they lack discernment to know how to appropriate what's being said. Their lack of intimacy with the Lord and hearing His voice for themselves can sometimes allow their insecurities to shut down the voice of the Lord. This is a Jezebel spirit using them and there is nothing worse (1 Kings 18.)

Giving prophetic words can be so fun and exciting. When done right, it encourages all involved. I am certain that as some of you read this, you have had times when you just *knew* something about someone that the Holy Spirit had revealed to you. This is Him sharing with you for the sake of prayer and possibly to share with that person.

Hearing personal things from the Holy Spirit and having the faith to speak it out as He tells us to takes courage. Fear to share it always tries to come in, too. What if we are wrong? What if they don't believe us? The truth is we have to be obedient to what we sense the Holy Spirit telling us and let it unfold. Many times, the Lord has me give an awkward word for someone and there is no choice for me but to be obedient and share it.

I once had to tell someone something very specific about them, wounds that others had done against them. The Lord said He would use them in another country with indigenous people and that healing would come to them and then pour through them for these other people. Years later I heard back from this person and indeed they ended up ministering to Native American people, in the area in which they too had been wounded. Only the Holy Spirit can give detailed words like that. Praise Him!

One time I was praying in a group over someone and the Holy Spirit showed me this person wearing a fisherman's hat with all the fishhooks and lures stuck in it. There were words God gave me to share along with this. It meant so much to this man, and ministered to him about something in his past. Only Jesus can do that. He has been faithful, over and over, all for His glory and to bless others. Still, it encourages my faith too. He loves us so much. But as you can see, our obedience and courage to speak what He tells us depends on our ability to hear Him and trust Him.

Often the Lord has used our children to speak to us. Children, if taught how to be still and pray, are the best at hearing from the Lord. My Son Jonah once came into our room in the night and said, "Mom, did you all call me?" He had heard his name being called several times and thought it was one of us. We realized that it was the Lord calling his name so I got up and sat in prayer with him. The Lord said nothing more to him but I believe was teaching Jonah how to hear His voice and respond, over time Jonah had several encounters with the Lord like this and some very profound. If children are taught to pay attention to the Lord, they will hear Him much easier than adults.

The Lord has also used our kids to correct us. One time my husband's grandmother was sick in the hospital. We were active on the mission field but living on the mainland and drove back to our home state to visit. We visited Grandmother in the hospital, prayed over her, and anointed her with oil as the Holy Spirit told us to. Afterwards, we were packing to leave and our son Micah came to us and said, "I don't think we are supposed to leave." We said we needed to get back, continued to pack and got on the road to head home. Micah said again in the car that he didn't think we were supposed to leave, Jonah also said that he too believed we were to not leave. Now, usually at this point we would have said, "Let's pray together and ask the

Lord," but because we were focused on getting home, we didn't. Three and a half hours into the trip we got a phone call that Grandmother had gone to be with the Lord. We pulled the car over and repented to the Lord for not listening. We also repented to our sons. Micah and Jonah were faithful to try and tell us. Kids are so sensitive to the Spirit's leading. The Lord has used our three sons countless times to speak to us. Praise His Name!

Prophetic dreams are another way the Holy Spirit speaks, as we read about in the lives of Daniel, Jeremiah, David, Joseph, John and more. Most people don't pay attention to their dreams but God speaks in powerful ways in our dreams. Sadly, when our mind is not submitted to the Holy Spirit, the enemy can come in on our dreams as well, giving us nightmares. What we watch and hear on TV, movies, and music also affects our dreams.

As you grow in your prayer life and learn to hear the Lord's voice, don't be surprised if you notice your dreams picking up, or your mind seeing pictures as you pray. Pay attention to them and be sure and submit these to the Lord. Ask Him about them. Some of them are just to encourage you and yet some will be from the flesh.

I've had many health issues but I don't let them define me. I've risen above them with a strong belief in the healing power of the Cross. I once had to have a procedure done in the hospital. Right before I was given the drugs for anesthesia, I prayed and asked the Lord to give me a sweet dream. Wow, He blessed me beyond words. I dreamt that I was walking the streets of Jerusalem. Jesus was taking me in and out of these homes within the town. He was showing them to me as if I could pick one of them to be mine. In the dream we heard a rumbling sound and hurried down to the street to see what it was. I saw in the distance a flood of pure gold coming down the street. It was sweeping from side to side, rushing like water, but it was GOLD! No one was getting hurt; it was just so beautiful and then as if I had speakers in my head I heard loudly the song *We Will Dance* by David Ruis.

> "We will dance on streets that are golden,
> the glorious Bride and the great Son of man.
> From every tongue and tribe and nation,
> We'll join, in the song of the Lamb."

Oh my, I have had many prophetic dreams but this one was personal, straight from Jesus and just for me. The Lord encouraged me with His promise that He is preparing a place for us, that there will be a New Jerusalem, New Heaven and Earth with streets of gold for His children to walk and dance. It was spectacular and these words can't do it justice. Thank you, Jesus!

Prophecy comes in many forms and it's all to encourage us. We are told by Paul to

"Pursue love, yet desire earnestly spiritual gifts, but especially that you may prophecy." – 1 Corinthians 14:1

I believe it was ultimately because Paul knew that real prophecy flows out of a love relationship with Jesus. The result of being in the stillness with Him is to love Him and one another. To prophesy, edify, exhort, and empower the Body of Christ is to truly change the world. And by this the world will know who Jesus is! (Psalms 46:10 and John 17)

18 – Closing with Joy

Consider it all joy, my brothers and sisters, when you encounter various trials, knowing that the testing of your faith produces endurance. – James 1:2-3

In closing I'd like to share on the joy that comes from being in the stillness with the Lord.

We are told we will certainly have heart aches, pain, affliction, trials and tribulations, but none are meant to destroy us. The Lord's trainings and teachings are to get us to finish the race and endure what this life brings. The devil means to destroy us, but Jesus has equipped us with everything we need to not only succeed but to defeat him. We are to protect our joy by spending time with Jesus. By doing this, the devil is forever a loser in our lives.

Jesus said, "My sheep hear my voice." He said this with great joy in His heart, not so we would feel inferior, or under condemnation, but so we would know what He has made available to us, and what we're capable of hearing.

"Fixing our eyes on Jesus, the author and perfecter of faith, who for the joy set before Him endured the cross, despising the shame, and has sat down at the right hand of the throne of God." – Hebrews 12:2

What a verse. Jesus was so fixed on what He needed to do out of His amazing love for us, that it brought Him joy to do it. He knew how it would truly give us the ability to conquer all obstacles the enemy would put in front of us. By the blood of the Lamb we were made new and able to partner with the Lion! We are now heirs to the throne of God where we will reign with Him forever. The sky is the limit for His children. As we sit in His presence, allowing Him to renew our hearts and minds so that we truly know just *who we are* in Jesus, there will be nothing we can't do according to His Word. Of course, joy comes with embracing our cross, and there is certainly pain attached to the crosses we carry. Yet, there is joy attached to picking up that cross out of our love and obedience to Jesus. Our joy is a true reflection of our obedience to Him.

I pray that you have been encouraged in your prayer life with the Lord. He loves you so deeply and so looks forward to daily spending time with you. He longs to show you things in the secret place with Him, things that are just between the two of you (Matthew 6:6.)

This life is precious but very temporary; your time with Jesus is eternal. Start fresh today with the Lord. No matter what kind of relationship you have with Him now, there is always more to be had and deeper to go. Take time now to renew that time with Him, asking Him for more of His personhood. He will be faithful to answer. Here is 1 Chronicles 16:8-36, a psalm of thanksgiving that is full of joy as well.

[8] Give thanks to the LORD, call upon His name;

Make His deeds known among the peoples.

[9] Sing to Him, sing praises to Him;

Speak of all His wonders.

[10] Boast in His holy name;

Let the heart of those who seek the LORD be joyful.

[11] Seek the LORD and His strength;

Seek His face continually.

[12] Remember His wonderful deeds which He has done,

His marvels and the judgments from His mouth,

[13] *You* descendants of Israel His servant,

Sons of Jacob, His chosen ones!

[14] He is the LORD our God;

His judgments are in all the earth.

[15] Remember His covenant forever,

The word which He commanded to a thousand generations,

[16] *The covenant* which He made with Abraham,

And His oath to Isaac.

[17] He also confirmed it to Jacob as a statute,

To Israel as an everlasting covenant,

[18] Saying, "To you I will give the land of Canaan,

As the portion of your inheritance."

¹⁹ When they were only a few in number,

Very few, and strangers in it,

²⁰ And they wandered from nation to nation,

And from *one* kingdom to another people,

²¹ He allowed no one to oppress them,

And He rebuked kings for their sakes, *saying*,

²² "Do not touch My anointed ones,

And do not harm My prophets."

²³ Sing to the LORD, all the earth;

Proclaim good news of His salvation from day to day.

²⁴ Tell of His glory among the nations,

His wonderful deeds among all the peoples.

²⁵ For great is the LORD, and greatly to be praised;

He also is to be feared above all gods.

²⁶ For all the gods of the peoples are idols,

But the LORD made the heavens.

²⁷ Splendor and majesty are before Him,

Strength and joy are in His place.

²⁸ Ascribe to the LORD, you families of the peoples,

Ascribe to the LORD glory and strength.

²⁹ Ascribe to the LORD the glory due His name;

Bring an offering, and come before Him;

Worship the LORD in holy attire.

³⁰ Tremble before Him, all the earth;

Indeed, the world is firmly established, it will not be moved.

³¹ Let the heavens be joyful, and the earth rejoice;

And let them say among the nations, "The LORD reigns."

³² Let the sea roar, and everything it contains;

Let the field rejoice, and everything that is in it.

³³ Then the trees of the forest will sing for joy in the presence
of the LORD;

For He is coming to judge the earth.

³⁴ Give thanks to the LORD, for *He is* good;

For His faithfulness is everlasting.

³⁵ Then say, "Save us, God of our salvation,

And gather us and save us from the nations,

To give thanks to Your holy name,

And glory in Your praise."

³⁶ Blessed be the LORD, the God of Israel,

From everlasting to everlasting!

Then all the people said, "Amen," and praised the LORD.

My Prayer for you:

Lord Jesus, I thank you for this person reading these words, and I pray right now for them. You know every detail in their life like no other person. You know every hurt, scar, and victory they have walked through. I ask from this day forward, that You would draw them into a deeper place with You; a deeper relationship with You like they have never known. I plead the blood of Jesus over them, their life, their home and their walk with You, that as the enemy comes to attack, they will remember You have equipped them to conquer all obstacles. I pray that the secret place in the stillness with You will become their favorite place to be and that nothing would keep them from it. May the Word of God become like the air they breathe, a daily necessity of life. Thank you, Jesus, for hearing my prayer. – Amen.

In the Stillness